"Ellen Vaughn has been a true friend in life's journey. In her I've seen the reality of faith in hard times and the joy of faith in a weary world. She cuts to real truth and hope in her writing, and also shows an enormous sense of the joy of the Lord. She makes me laugh."

GREG LAURIE
Award-winning author and senior pastor of
Harvest Christian Fellowship (Riverside, CA)

"What a privilege it is for me to endorse Ellen Vaughn's book. Matthew 11:28 has long been a favorite of mine, but now I understand it in a much deeper way. Ellen is such a gifted communicator because she is authentic. *Come, Sit, Stay* is extremely insightful, humorous, and impactful. You will want to pass this book on."

RON BLUE
Best-selling author, president of Kingdom Advisors,
founder of Ronald Blue & Co.

"I've always loved Jesus' invitation to come to Him, we who are weary and burdened, and find rest for our souls. This refreshing book is a great tool to understand more deeply the radical rest that only Jesus can give, and the shimmering, eternal perspective that can actually bring deep peace, right in the midst of our busy days. Ellen is a witty, clear writer, and *Come, Sit, Stay* is a fast, compelling read."

JONI EARECKSON TADA
Founder of Joni and Friends and best-selling author

"Ellen Vaughn is brilliant, insightful, funny, Christ-loving, and has a dog named after C. S. Lewis. But to top it off, she is also a terrific writer. I've enjoyed and benefited from Ellen's books for many years."

RANDY ALCORN
Best-selling author and founder of Eternal Perspective Ministries

"Life today is fired point-blank. To any left frazzled by the speed, stuff, and stress of our 24/7 fast-life, Ellen Vaughn's meditations are a beautiful invitation to discover rest in the midst of modern craziness."

OS GUINNESS
Author of The Call

"Ellen Vaughn is a gifted, persuasive, and sometimes blunt writer who understands how both humor and story can winsomely disarm us and reveal truths we may have sought to avoid. Her book is a refreshing invitation to consider Christ's tender words to the weary and a balm for our disquieted souls."

DR. RAVI ZACHARIAS
Author and speaker

"I love the idea of coming sitting, and staying with Jesus, and finding real rest for the soul. Ellen Vaughn is able to communicate deep spiritual truths while humbly and authentically relating to her readers in a winsome way."

JOANNE KEMP
Washington study group leader and widow of former Congressman, Cabinet member, and vice presidential candidate Jack Kemp

"This is an invigorating book, not about religion, but about a relationship with the surprising God who invites us to come to Him and be uniquely refreshed. Ellen Vaughn has captured essential truths in unusual ways; this is a fun read that goes deep."

ERIC METAXAS
New York Times *best-selling author of* Bonhoeffer: Pastor, Martyr, Prophet, Spy *and* Amazing Grace: William Wilberforce and the Heroic Campaign to End Slavery

"Ellen Vaughn at her inimitable, punchy, lyrical, biblical, practical, helpful best. With a lightness of touch, she shows us what rest for our souls is all about."

ALISTAIR BEGG
Senior pastor of Parkside Church (Cleveland, OH), daily teacher on "Truth for Life," author

Come,
Sit, Stay

ELLEN VAUGHN

NEW YORK TIMES BEST-SELLING AUTHOR

Come, Sit, Stay

finding rest for your soul

An Invitation to a Deeper Life in Christ

WORTHY
PUBLISHING

to
Dois Rosser
and
Chuck Colson

*fathers, brothers, mentors in Christ
who woke my dozing heart and mind*

Come to me, all you who are weary and burdened,
and I will give you rest.
Take my yoke upon you
and learn from me,
for I am gentle and humble in heart,
and you will find rest
for your souls.
For my yoke is easy
and my burden is light.
MATTHEW 11:28–30

{Contents}

Come
{to grace}

sit
{pay attention!}

stay
{obey}

rest
{trust and blessing}

{Foreword}

I've known Ellen Vaughn for many years. I can't remember if we first met in prison or not. If so, it wasn't because of crimes we had committed, but because of our mutual involvement with Chuck Colson and the grace-filled work that Prison Fellowship has brought to so many prisoners and prisons everywhere.

Or maybe we met in Nashville, through mutual friends. It may have been during a time when her husband, Lee, was doing some work with our organization, Show Hope. Whatever the case, I remember realizing that this was THE Ellen Vaughn who had been a part of writing some of my favorite Chuck Colson books, and I was impressed! However, after spending just a little time with her, I recognized Ellen as a kindred spirit . . . a person who loves Jesus, loves words, loves friends, and has a wonderful (and maybe just a bit wacky) sense of humor.

Because of this, I talked with Ellen a number of years ago about us doing a book together. She and Mary Beth and I ate biscuits and chicken and fried okra for lunch at our favorite Franklin (Tennessee) restaurant. We talked that day about the story God was telling in our lives. We dreamed about what He might be doing. We planned to reconvene later to perhaps write a book.

I had no idea the form that book would take. I could not have known that it would in fact grow out of devastating tragedy. But on May 21, 2008, our Chapman story changed forever, when our youngest daughter, Maria, went to be with Jesus as the result of a terrible accident at our home a week after her fifth birthday.

In our awful loss, so many people around the world supported us through their prayers. Somehow God held us in our grief. Somehow our faith held too. And in the ashes of our pain, we believed God had given us a "sacred trust" to share His reality and His plans for good in the midst of what Satan had intended for evil.

It seemed unthinkable to write a book about such a ripping loss. But God worked in Mary Beth's heart, and she made the courageous decision to do so. We both believed that God could use our broken story to show His healing power. Mary Beth was willing to lay herself wide open, if that's what it took, so others might see God's amazing grace.

And in those painful days, it was also natural—if I can use that word—for us to turn to Ellen Vaughn. We knew Ellen would help shepherd our story faithfully, with a sense of God's sovereignty and of our own deep pain. We believed she could come alongside us in the midst of dark times and make God's story come alive.

Ellen did that. She entered into our world. She embraced the craziness of the Chapman family, with people running every which way with wild schedules. She spent time with our sons, helped our younger daughters with their homework, ate Ramen noodles in our family room, and came to Shaoey's basketball games. We listened to her go on about flamingos in *Alice in Wonderland* and great literature throughout the ages. (Remember that wacky sense of humor I told you about?) She listened while we laughed and cried and did everything in between. She helped clarify events and wrestled through tough issues with Mary Beth. We ate many egg salad sandwiches together. As Mary Beth would say, Ellen was an amazing "birthing coach" for her as she "labored" to tell her story, and the result of it all was Mary Beth's beautifully and painfully honest book, *Choosing to SEE.*

So, if I may say so, Mary Beth and I love and trust Ellen Vaughn. She seeks a real, radical relationship with Jesus, and this book you're holding is part of the fruit of her quest. I was deeply encouraged as I read it. She lives in what we often call the "real world," although I would submit that heaven is actually the Real world and this earthly experience is just the Shadowlands, as C. S. Lewis called it. But what I mean is, she's not an armchair philosopher. She writes and lives and breathes and struggles with faith in the midst of busy chaos, just like you and me . . . and the result is words on a page that somehow ring True, that help us all to lift our faces to the One who loves us more than we can imagine—the One who can offer real rest for our weary souls.

Steven Curtis Chapman
On a plane somewhere between Nashville and Belfast,
April 19, 2012

Come

{to grace}

1
{Frisky Love}

Man interferes with the dog and makes it more lovable than it was in mere nature. . . . He washes it, housetrains it. . . . To the puppy the whole proceeding would seem, if it were a theologian, to cast grave doubts on the "goodness" of man: but the full-grown and full-trained dog, . . . admitted, as it were by Grace, to a whole world of affections, loyalties, interests and comforts entirely beyond its animal destiny, would have no such doubts.

We may wish, indeed, that we were of so little account to God that He left us alone to follow our natural impulses—that He would give over trying to train us into something so unlike our natural selves: but once again, we are asking not for more Love, but for less.

C. S. Lewis, *The Problem of Pain*

This book began when I was walking along the beach a while ago. The waves shimmered with the light of the sun, the sand was warm, and the sea gulls rode the wind. All was well . . . except for me. I was carrying heavy burdens, torn up inside, exhausted and desperate and numb, all at the same time. I was thinking about a difficult situation I'd prayed about a thousand times, wondering if it would ever end. You've probably felt that way. I stared at the sea, soothed by its rise and fall, and then my mind locked in on some of the most well-known words of Scripture.

"Come to Me, all you who are weary and burdened, and I will give you rest."

That kind invitation from Jesus is so familiar that I usually skip right over it. *Yep, I know that. Cool. I really need to think about it sometime when I have more time.*

But pain has a way of concentrating the mind. As I walked, I actually focused on Jesus' invitation. I took it apart, word-by-word-by-word, chewing on it, meditating on it. I walked on, looking out over God's good ocean, and that old verse from Matthew 11 became real in a new way. I saw a glimpse of Jesus; I heard His invitation to come. I could almost see His arms open wide. I felt His grace. This wasn't about me being "good enough" to come; it was all about His love. A kaleidoscope of color and meaning swirled from His words. I smelled a whiff of sea-breeze hope. Tears rolled down my face.

And for the first time in a long time, I felt rest and refreshment for my soul.

Happily, I found that I didn't have to be at the ocean to experience this. Back home in suburbia, I'd be sitting at my desk, or in traffic, or standing in my kitchen full of hungry, dysfunctional teenagers, and Jesus' words would actually come back to me and give me rest. I found that I could "come" to Him no matter where I was, no matter how stuck or stressed I felt. I could experience the peace of a secure relationship with Him, right in the midst of chaos or crisis.

As I reflected on this happy development, I realized I had been missing a great blessing—a wonderful gift that's worth sharing—and so I wrote this book.

Perhaps you're like me. Perhaps you originally came to Jesus and felt great freedom as He eased your load. But maybe, over the course of the journey with Him, your burdens piled up and you lost your joy. It happens so easily: we unconsciously lose our focus on Christ and begin to look to ourselves. We distractedly go through the routines of the "Christian life," whatever that is, depending on our own strength, discipline, and works. It's as if we know that we're saved by grace, yes, but we act like our sanctification—the process of becoming more and more like Christ—is up to us and our efforts.

When that happens, the world goes gray. The bright colors and fun vitality of an intimate relationship with Jesus fade to an anxious, resentful, weary, and burdened religious life: the very thing Jesus came to free people from.

Or perhaps you've never come to Jesus in the first place, and you are weary and burdened by all kinds of stuff. In that case there's great news here, because embedded within Jesus' call to "come to Me" is a progression of verbs that actually lead to the result of rest. Wonderful, real, rest for our souls. And if you have a strange brain like me, these verbs happen to sound a lot like dog commands. I'm not suggesting that we're all retrievers or poodles or border collies . . . but I am saying that there is a certain frisky love, power, and freedom in obedience that is unleashed when we respond to Jesus' invitation and learn to obey the commands of the Master.

Come.

Sit.

Stay.

And when we obey these commands, the rich result is *rest.*

The rest that Jesus gives isn't about lying on a hammock somewhere in the Caribbean, although that sounds pretty great right about now. But you know that you can be prone in a hammock, sipping a frosted fruit smoothie, your body in repose—and your soul can feel as weary and burdened as ever. A lovely environment alone cannot give rest. If that was the case, everyone in Hollywood or the Riviera or Vail and Aspen would be peaceful, and I can't help but notice that many are not. If I may make a generalization, many people I've met who have come to Jesus and live in tin-roofed shacks in developing nations have a lot more "rest" than many wealthy, restless people who are far from Him.

The benefits of a good night's sleep or an amazing massage that actually makes you whimper last only so long, and then the world and its worries intrude again, wrecking your so-called "karma" and knotting your muscles all over again.

True rest is something far more mysterious. The way Jesus said it in the original language was "I will rest you." As we'll see later,

Jesus wasn't just expressing a nice Hallmark card-type sentiment. His claim to be able to give people rest when they come to Him is rooted in the fact that He is God. He has all authority and power on heaven and earth. He can do miracles. He can rest us, in a supernatural, soothing, counterintuitive peace in the midst of any conflict, frustration, or challenge. In fact, His call to "come" *promises* rest . . . an assurance only God Almighty can make.

This rest can change our lives. It can free us from the anxious activity and relentless striving that keeps many believers in a shallow performance mentality and robs them of real, deep freedom and rest in Christ.

For those who come to Jesus, His next command is simple: "Sit!"

When I say this to my dog Gus, he is usually quite compliant. He'll park his furry bottom right away. But because his brain is small and cluttered, he is easily distracted. Often after obediently sitting for a moment, he'll pop right back up and amble away to do all the other things he thinks he should be doing, like looking for crumbs on the kitchen floor.

There's not one particular verse to cite here, but if you look at Jesus' teaching, you'll see the pattern. He tells His people to sit . . . not because He thinks we're robots or have been to dog obedience school, but because in order to learn who He really is, human beings need to "sit down and count the cost" (Luke 14:28 ESV) of following Him.

The Gospels also repeatedly say that Jesus told the crowds to "sit down" so they could listen to Him for a while. For us, this means choosing to give our most precious commodity—time—

to sit down and read the Bible. Not speed reading, but digesting the Scriptures, chewing on them thoughtfully.

"Sitting" also means choosing to spend time praying, meditating, being still, and communing with God through the power of the Holy Spirit. This communion is wild, transcendent, supernatural . . . yet it comes not through some celestial cosmic convergence, but through simple, practical decisions on our part. Spiritual disciplines essentially boil down to "sitting" at Jesus' feet, so to speak. This can't be done on the run, downloaded in a few seconds, or swallowed like an instant holy pill.

When I think of "sitting," I think of Jesus' friend Mary of Bethany. You remember the story of the first-century twisted sisters who were hosting Jesus and His disciples for a dinner party. Martha was running around supervising servants, wringing chickens' necks, folding all her linen napkins into elegant, angry swans, sweating, stressed . . . and she got more and more livid as the evening went on.

Mary, meanwhile, was literally "sitting at Jesus' feet," the Bible says. This was a Jewish term for how students would take in the teachings of a rabbi. She was learning of Him.

It's far easier to identify with Martha, who was busy getting stuff done. Many of us have always secretly thought that Mary was a weenie, and we've wondered why Jesus said that she had made the better choice. We would never admit that, of course, because it would sound unspiritual. But the simple fact was that Mary had discovered the way to get to know her friend Jesus was to sit with Him, and that was a higher priority for her than running around like a crazy woman.

This sitting thing is radically countercultural in our day of constant hurry, productivity, multitasking, and busyness. It requires the intentional choice to be with Jesus, not just sitting for only a moment like my distractable dog, but spending *time* with Him.

As you would guess, the third command that Jesus gives those He has already called to "come" and "sit" is this: "Stay!"

This is hard. As I've said, when I tell Gus to sit, he does, but then he soon gets distracted by other things. And when I tell him to "stay," he'll hang with me for a moment, and then he wanders away.

I do the same thing with God. I'm "prone to wander," as the old hymn puts it, "prone to leave the God I love." I wander even though I *know* He's my Master.

When Christ had been teaching some hard truths and a lot of people who had been following Him decided to get off the Jesus bus, He asked His closest disciples, *Are you guys going to leave Me too?*

Peter responded, "Lord, to whom shall we go? You have the words of eternal life, and we have believed, and have come to know, that you are the Holy One of God" (John 6:68–69 ESV).

I love that. But it's possible to marvel over that wonderful verse and agree with it totally in your head and then still wander away anyway, like a dumb sheep. I know. I've done it. Come to think of it, so did Peter in his dysfunctional days before Jesus' resurrection.

Just before His crucifixion, Jesus told His friends to stay with Him. He said over and over to His disciples, as recorded in John

15, remain in Me, abide in Me, *stay* with Me: "I am the vine; you are the branches. If you remain in me and I in you, you will bear much fruit; apart from me you can do nothing" (John 15:5). The Greek verb used is *meno*, which means to stay, remain, live, dwell, abide.

This is an active verb . . . not passive. Staying with Jesus is never passive. It is not like when a dog stays on the doormat while his master leaves to go out and do important things. It is like riding in a cavalry with a general who shouts to his soldiers over the fray, "Stay with me! *Stay* with me!" It is galloping, straining, exulting, and keeping pace with the One who is in charge.

COME, SIT, and STAY are active verbs of *ingress*, or the way *in* to Jesus. Taken together, they lead us to true rest for our souls . . . an incredible gift, given the wearisome nature of the burdens we carry.

Many books encourage us to set out on certain steps to spirituality. This is great . . . but perhaps the idea of steps to a deeper faith puts the focus on the steppers—us—rather than on the personality and power of God Himself. *Come, Sit, Stay* seeks to focus on the nature of God. That's too huge a topic to be contained in all the books of the world, let alone my feeble efforts. But I take comfort in God's tendency to reveal Himself through small means . . . just as He calls everybody, anybody, large or small, to Himself.

2

{Royal Invitation, Legal Summons, Radical Rescue}

Christ's voice sounds now for each of us in loving invitation;
and dead in sin and hardness of heart though we be,
we can listen and live.
Christ Himself, my brother, sows the seed now.
Do you take care that it falls not on, but in, *your souls?*

ALEXANDER MACLAREN,
"The Seed by the Wayside" sermon

I've always thought it would be helpful if the United States had a royal family. It would take a big burden off the president.

In our system of government, the presidency is a huge and serious role that gives gray hair to whoever holds the job. The poor president not only has to be commander-in-chief and chief executive, lead his party, deal with Congress, and beat his brains out on issues and approval ratings, but as head of state he or she has to do ceremonial jobs. A lot of these official tasks fall to the spouse, so you'll see First Ladies christening battleships and dedicating parks . . . but people still expect their president to light the national Christmas tree, throw out the first ball of the baseball season, roll out the first egg at the White House Easter Egg Roll, and proclaim National Seat Belt Day.

But as nice as it is to see the president participate in these lovely events, they take a lot of time and energy. Just think, if we had a queen or king, the royals could do all the ceremonial tasks, freeing the president to concentrate on the big stuff. The focus could be on the queen's wardrobe, and everyone could leave the First Lady alone about which designers she likes. Instead of people crashing White House state dinners, they could go after royal dinners, and the president and whatever head of state is visiting could just order carryout and keep working on world peace.

And *Entertainment Tonight*-type questions could go to the king or queen. This way we wouldn't have things like some years ago when Bill Clinton was interviewed by MTV and asked if he preferred boxers or briefs. This is just the wrong question for people to be asking the leader of the free world. It doesn't play well in Pretoria or Pakistan. But if we had a royal family, human-interest queries could go to them instead . . . and few reporters would likely ask royals about their underwear anyway.

The royal family could also be the focus for our need for ritual, pomp, and circumstance. Rather than bothering the White House, the entertainment media could go crazy over elaborate ceremonies at the palace.

For example, think back to Great Britain's wedding of Prince William and Kate Middleton . . . an enormous media frenzy, watched by two billion people around the world.

Due to space constraints in Westminster Abbey, only about 1,900 select folks received the elegant, gold-stamped invitation to the wedding. Engraved with the royal crest, it began, "The Lord Chamberlain is commanded by the Queen to invite" so-and-so. To their credit, William and Kate invited commoners as well as royalty and high-society icons . . . but there were a lot of big so-and-sos who didn't make the cut, a lot of important noses left out of joint. Why was Elton John invited, but not Madonna? Why did the president of France and his wife receive the royal invitation, but not the president of the United States?

In this world, such invitations would not mean as much if they were not exclusive. You wouldn't have gate-crashers at galas or security and bouncers at high-level parties if *everyone* was invited. The cachet of the event depends on how elite and selective it is.

Usually earthly kings, queens, Hollywood royalty, presidents, and CEOs invite only those who have enough money, influence, power, beauty, or brains to qualify for an invitation. You just don't see people without connections at the soirees of Washington, New York, LA, or Paris. And you don't see a lot of unattractive guests at Oscar parties, unless they are wealthy or brilliant. (I would submit, also, that there are few unattractive women. Ugly rich men, yes, but never unappealing women. What's up with that?)

But God's royal invitation is different. He breaks this world's rules. He issues His golden call to people who have precisely nothing to offer, people who feel worthless, downtrodden. He invites the poor, the disabled, the weak and needy.

But He doesn't stop there. In some sort of reverse discrimination, He wants everybody to come to His party. He invites not just the poor and weary, but also the rich and strong, and everyone in between.

There is a bubbling-over passion about God's call, the sense that He is so crazy about us that He just doesn't care that His invitation is pretty radical. Come one and all!

Of course, Jesus' words are not just an invitation. They are also, in a way, a summons coming from the ultimate royalty, though He didn't look like a king. Few people invited by a king turn him down. In past centuries, declining a sovereign's invitation—aka summons—would cause you to lose your head.

Again, since we don't have royalty in the United States, perhaps the better image is of a court summons. A summons is not an Evite. You don't get to click *yes, no,* or *maybe I'll come, depending on how I feel.*

Just the other day our wonderful teenaged son got a ticket for reckless driving. He's not a reckless youth, but he just happened to be proceeding at a rate of fifty miles per hour in his high school zone. A nice police officer was kind enough to stop him and inform him that the speed limit there is twenty-five.

So Walker came home not with just a speeding ticket, which is scary enough, but a summons. It's a yellow paper covered with menacing small print and legal language. It is not an invitation. It says, "You must appear at trial." Period. Walker will show up, in court, before a judge, on the particular date and time of the judge's bidding. It's a command performance.

Now, Walker has a choice, I suppose. But the course of wisdom is to obey the summons, lest more dire consequences follow from both the court and his loving parents.

Jesus' call to us is less threatening. But if we think about it, it has the same force of law, spiritually speaking. He invites us now, summons us now, calls us to come. We do have a choice. But the day will come, at the end of all things, when every person on the planet *will* come to Jesus, *compelled* to appear before Him. To those who chose to come and receive Him, whose names are written in the Book of Life, He'll say, *Come on in to heaven and its eternal delights.*

To those who chose not to come to Him, He'll say those sad words: "Depart from Me, for I never knew you" (see Matthew 7:23). As C. S. Lewis put it, "There are only two kinds of people in the end: those who say to God, 'Thy will be done,' and those to whom God says, in the end, 'Thy will be done.' All that are in Hell, choose it. Without that self-choice there could be no Hell. No soul that seriously and constantly desires joy will ever miss it. Those who seek find. To those who knock it is opened."[1]

To change the picture from the summons, think about calling a dog to come. It's a basic command.

Though it is rare for our dog Gus to be obedient, there is great joy in Vaughn World when he is. Gus is a whoodle, the result of a love match between a poodle and a wheaten terrier. He is a quivering mass of Rastafarian fur, enthusiasm, and energy. I love when we're outside and he's far away and I call him and he actually comes. He runs and leaps and bounds like a furry gazelle, running as fast as he can, ears flapping, teeth grinning, happy, happy dog.

Sometimes when I call Gus to come, it's not just by whim. It's because I see danger that he does not.

For example, we had an earthquake the other day in Washington, DC. Now, lots of things happen in Washington, but earthquakes are not one of them. This was a first for me.

I was upstairs in our house. Suddenly I heard what sounded like a jet flying low overhead or a train rumbling by. My house was shaking. I could hear things falling off the walls and glass breaking as vases toppled to the floor.

I couldn't quite register what was happening. Then a teeny little file in my brain popped open. It was labeled "earthquake." For a moment I couldn't remember if I was supposed to get in a doorway, or under a heavy table, or run in zigzags . . . oh, wait, that's what you're supposed to do when a crocodile is chasing you.

Anyway, my disaster response neurons were all firing, and I flew down the front stairs. Gus was frozen in confusion, his eyes wild and his body shaking. "COME!" I yelled. "Gus, COME!"

He flew down the stairs after me, we ran toward the front door, and Gus and I escaped to the safety of the front yard.

I called Gus to come with great urgency. I recognized the danger he could not perceive.

It's rare to call an adult person and get the same response. The only time adults hurry when you call them is if they understand they're in danger.

Let me illustrate.

Like most people my age, my life was skewed forever by the original *Jaws* movie, which came out when I was in college. Before seeing *Jaws*, I could swim in the ocean without a thought. But after *Jaws*, every time I was in the surf, all I could think about were all those underwater shots in the movie where you see people in the water from the shark's perspective. All those legs, dangling like juicy hors d'oeuvres. People lying on rafts like open-faced sandwiches. In most of the movie, it was a day at the beach for the giant shark, an all-you-can-eat buffet.

I've always been a person with a strong imagination. My *Jaws*-phobia made me uneasy even when I was swimming in freshwater lakes . . . but I wasn't quite as bad as my college roommate, who had seen the movie and was in the dorm late one night, reading *Jaws* the book.

Transfixed, she suddenly became aware, in her peripheral vision, of a large, menacing shape that looked just like a killer shark's gray, conical snout. Screaming, Patti woke the rest of us up, terrified and traumatized by the shark-like threat of what she had seen out of the corner of her eye: yes, our *ironing board*.

As you know, the *Jaws* sequels got progressively worse—in one of them the shark actually takes down a helicopter—but at any rate, I digress.

So here's my point. In the original *Jaws* there's a scene where a reward has been offered for killing the killer shark. Two guys go out to bring it in. They're not too bright, perhaps; they are fishing for this shark off a dock, and one has taken his wife's dinner roast out of the refrigerator for bait.

The two guys toss the roast out on the water, attached to a heavy chain that is secured to the dock, with a floating inner tube as a bobber. "Come and get it!" they yell. (They don't know they are dealing with the mega-monster shark of the century.)

The shark, who likes dinner roasts, seizes the bait. The chain holds, and as the shark takes his dinner out to sea, he pulls half the pier out with him. The two men fall off the broken pier and into the water.

One of them manages to scramble onto the remaining portion of the dock, but his partner, Charlie, is still in the water. Then we see the broken part of the pier—attached to the roast, attached to the shark—ominously reverse direction. For the shark, the roast was the appetizer; now he wants Charlie for the main course.

Charlie knows that all is not well, but he doesn't see the giant shark approaching from behind him. His friend does. He's yelling, "Come on, Charlie! Swim! Swim! Come on!!!!"

That's the kind of urgency that is in Jesus' call to us. Even if we are unaware, He sees the danger and gravity of our situation without Him. He alone can rescue us. And so He calls . . . "Come! Come! *Now!*"

In the New Testament, Jesus called all kinds of people to come and follow Him: broken-down sinners, proud religious people, children, skeptics, and people who desperately needed real love.

He does the same today. He makes the first move. In the Greek verb form that was used in Matthew's Gospel, it's an imperative: "Come!"

He still gives us a choice. We can stay away. But if we do come to Him, it's the beginning of a new life that lasts forever and a new relationship with a new master.

3

{Who Is the Master?}

Under the bludgeonings of chance
My head is bloody, but unbowed.

Beyond this place of wrath and tears
Looms but the Horror of the shade,
And yet the menace of the years
Finds and shall find me unafraid.

It matters not how strait the gate,
How charged with punishments the scroll,
I am the master of my fate:
I am the captain of my soul.

WILLIAM ERNEST HENLEY, *"Invictus"*

No one can serve two masters.
Either you will hate the one and love the other, or you will be
devoted to the one and despise the other.

MATTHEW 6:24

For many of us, "master" is a loaded, offensive, archaic term. It smacks of slavery at worst and *I Dream of Jeannie* at best. If you're too young to remember that cheesy old TV show, it was about an astronaut who found a bottle, brought it home, and when he rubbed it, a beautiful blond genie popped out. Her name was Jeannie, of course. She wore a weird pink harem outfit, and she was always perky and ready to do his bidding. She called him "Master."

Okay, that's ridiculous, even though it did come from the golden age of television.

What else does "master" bring to mind? Maybe an obedient dog, eyes fixed on its master. While I would submit there's something to work with there, most people just don't want to be a dog.

And certainly, there are far more severe and awful mental images of masters and slaves. We think of the horrors of the slave trade, with human beings bought and sold like cattle, though treated far worse. We think of shackles, repression, brutality, and injustice in earlier centuries . . . and of the cruelty of modern-day sex trafficking, the enslavement of young girls and boys all over the world.

Further, beyond these horrible mental images of slavery, Americans do not like the notion of mastery by anyone. In our Bibles, the term *doulos*—used many, many times to describe the relationship between us and Christ—is translated "bondservant." Its real, first-century meaning was more blunt: "slave."[1] For modern-day readers, that just doesn't compute. We are a people shaped by independence and self-sufficiency. We bend the knee to no one. In the cultural twenty-first-century understanding of our heritage, that's come to mean we are a people of total autonomy, dependent on and answering only to ourselves.

So we don't call anyone "master." How horrible.

But the plain fact is that human beings *will* be mastered by something or someone. Sorry. Many are mastered by things they think they control, but that in fact control them. Career. Fame. Position. Money. Worry. A relationship. A desire to be perceived in a certain way by others: smart, beautiful, witty, spiritual, successful. Whatever. In its most obvious manifestations, a master can be a substance like alcohol, drugs, or food—something that controls the person enslaved to it.

Some of us may feel like the hero of the famous poem "Invictus": Hey, "*I* am the master of my fate: I am the captain of my soul."[2]

Written in 1875 by a man who had endured terrible physical suffering all his life, the poem has inspired many. It encouraged former South African president Nelson Mandela throughout his prison term during his country's darkest days; director Clint Eastwood used it as the title for his popular film about the South African rugby team.

Sadly, it was also a great influence on Oklahoma City bomber Timothy McVeigh, who was responsible for the deaths of 186 men, women, and children, and the injuries of 800 more. He scribbled out the words of "Invictus" and handed this to authorities as his last words before his execution.

The poem is usually perceived in pop culture as an heroic stance . . . while it is essentially, as British journalist Daniel Hannan has observed, "a final and terrible act of defiance. The Horror might indeed have awaited him, but he would go there on his own terms, leaving the spittle sliding down his Maker's face."[3]

In its most entertaining manifestation, this mind-set of *oneself* as ultimate master can end up sounding like actor Charlie Sheen, who went through a much-publicized rant after his television network fired him. The media quotes were odd and mesmerizing:

> On his most recent drug binge: "I'm proud of what I created. It was radical. I exposed people to magic. I exposed them to something they're never going to see in their boring normal lives."

> On erratic behavior: "You borrow my brain for five seconds and just be like, dude, can't handle it, unplug this [thing]. It fires in a way that is, I don't know, maybe not from this terrestrial realm. When you've got tiger blood and Adonis DNA, it's like, get with the program, dude."

> On passing his drug test: "I am on a drug. It's called 'Charlie Sheen!' It's not available because if you try it once, you will die. Your face will melt off and your children will weep over your exploded body. . . . I'm tired of pretending I'm not special. I'm tired of pretending I'm not a total [freaking] rock star from Mars. People can't figure me out. They can't process me. I don't expect them to. You can't process me with a normal brain."[4]

Well, even when some of us glory in the fact that we are master of our own spaceship, accountable to no one, that can be the worst slavery of all. For my part, I think this mastery thing boils down to a basic choice: *Who do I really want to be in charge? Who do I want to be captain of my soul? Me—or Jesus? Will I come to Him or not?*

I love the closing words of the great British preacher Charles Spurgeon's very last sermon on June 7, 1891. He acknowledged a different "captain of the soul" than self.

> If you could see our Captain, you would go down on your knees and beg Him to let you enter the ranks of those who follow Him. It is heaven to serve Jesus. I am a recruiting sergeant, and I would rejoice to find a few recruits at this moment.
>
> Every [person] must serve somebody: we have no choice as to that fact. Those who have no master are slaves to themselves. Depend upon it, you will either serve Satan or Christ. Either self, or the Savior. You will find sin, self, Satan, and the world to be hard masters; but if you wear the uniform of Christ, you will find Him so meek and lowly of heart that you will find *rest* unto your souls.[5]

4

{Jesus Calling: Expectations vs. Reality}

The longer you look at Jesus,
the more you will want to serve him in this world.
That is, of course, if it's the real Jesus you're looking at.

N. T. WRIGHT, *Following Jesus*

Jesus issued a lot of "come" invitations during His time on earth.

Let the little children come to Me!

Anyone who is thirsty, come to Me and drink!

Come, follow Me!

Come, all you who are hungry!

And, of course, *Come to Me, all you who are weary and burdened!*

This is recorded in Matthew's Gospel, chapter 11. At this point Jesus was about thirty years old. He'd been a carpenter, living in Nazareth, flying under the radar. But now the time had come for Him to jump into public ministry and reveal Himself to those who had eyes to see and ears to hear.

He had been baptized by John the Baptist, one of the few people in the Bible whose name was also his job description, although I guess "Rahab the harlot" also qualifies. John had later been thrown into prison by the evil king Herod for the capital crime of pointing out the immorality of Herod's adulterous personal life.

Awaiting execution, John sent some of his friends with a question for Jesus. John had thought that the Jewish Messiah would come with great passion and force to overthrow Rome and establish the Jewish nation in its fullness. Jesus wasn't quite doing that. He was doing great things—healing people, preaching a whole new way of living and relating to God—but He was not kicking out the Romans and ushering in a new political kingdom.

So John, a dedicated, courageous man of God, had expectations about Jesus that just weren't being fulfilled. He was asking: Was Jesus the Messiah? Or not?

Meanwhile the Pharisees—the religious leaders and legalists

of the day—had their own preconceptions. Like all Jews, they believed that Messiah would come and save His people. Perhaps they thought He would be a fastidious rule-keeper with a small heart, a pointy nose, and beady, suspicious eyes. Just like them. They demanded that the common people keep unkeepable laws. Many of them were hypocrites who professed a holy lifestyle while they lived with hearts full of pride and indifference.

They claimed to be anxiously awaiting their Savior but did not recognize Him when He was standing right in front of them. Why? Jesus didn't meet their expectations. He just didn't look or act like they thought He would. He was too loving, too lavish, and way too fun.

There were also whole villages—with names like Capernaum, Bethsaida, and Chorazin—where Jesus had done all kinds of supernatural wonders earlier in His ministry. Certainly they would recognize their Messiah by His miracles!

Nope.

So in this section of Matthew's historical record, Jesus responds to some of these unmet assumptions. He tells John's friends to carry the word back to the first Baptist that He, Jesus, is the expected One, even though He doesn't look like what John had anticipated.

To the Pharisees, he essentially says, "You guys are never satisfied . . . you didn't like John the Baptist because he was too weird and ascetic; you don't like Me because I'm too 'worldly.'"

To the towns that had rejected Him, Jesus said, "Whoa, bad times are coming because you did not have the humility and repentance to recognize Me."

You don't have to be a first-century Jew to have false expectations about the Messiah. Many of us have our twenty-first-century assumptions of who Jesus is, often focused on what He will do for us. He'll make our lives go smoothly. He will heal my daughter or my son. He will give me a husband or fix the husband I have. He will give me a good job and success. He will make my cancer go into remission.

These desires are good things. Of course. But even though God has promised to give us the "desires of our hearts," His outcomes don't always match our natural desires. He has bigger fish to fry than our immediate relief. He is operating according to a perspective of eternity, and we are so easily limited by the perspective of our lives right now. He will bring good. He will redeem. All *shall* be well—even though we may not see that right now.

And sometimes our expectations can be more self-centered, as in these kinds of thoughts: *Jesus will help me to become more successful. He will protect me from discomfort and distress.* Even if we're not subscribing to an obvious health-and-wealth gospel that says Jesus will make you rich and thin and prosperous or all your efforts successful (in the world's terms), it's so easy to unconsciously expect that Jesus will cause our dreams to come true.

If we look at the history of people God blessed and called, including Jesus Christ Himself, we won't usually see ease in this life. Instead, we see a whole heap 'o trouble, as they used to say—difficulties, persecution, discomfort, trials—with great ease and wealth and health waiting in the life to come.

Meanwhile, in this life, many will quote—rightly—that *God*

will cause all things to work together for good, as Romans 8:28 says, *to give us a future and a hope,* as Jeremiah 29:11 puts it. Those great verses are true. But they are often quoted just in part, and the problem is, it's so easy for us to define our own terms of what the "good" or the "hope" looks like.

And when the outcomes we want don't happen, then it's easy to be put out: "Hey, what's going on here? Who is this Jesus, anyway, and what *is* His plan?"

Any time we ask that earnestly, it's a good thing.

I find that even though I've "known" Jesus most of my life, the older I get, the more I see how my natural tendency is to reduce Him to an image in my head.

If I may use an illustration put forth by Mark Dever and passed along by John Piper, it's like I have an idea of Jesus in my mind. So do you, and so does the next person. It's as if old classmates from college are discussing a common friend from thirty years earlier. The classmates begin to wonder if they are talking about the same person. One of them is convinced they are, and another keeps thinking this is not quite the way he remembers the friend. Finally, they decide to dig out an old yearbook and settle the issue.

They open the book, and as soon as they see the picture of their classmate, one says, "No, that's not who I am talking about." So it was not the same person after all.

Jesus, as He is revealed in the Bible, is the picture in the yearbook, according to Dever.[1] When people of different faith traditions—or, I would submit, Christians who have made up various pictures of Jesus in their heads—are discussing whether they are worshiping the same God, we need to look at God in the year-book, i.e., the Scriptures. That will settle the matter. "Oh," one might say, "now I realize I was seeing Him differently. That's not who He is at all."

Left to myself, it's so easy to be swayed by the culture out there and the confusing sin inside me. It's easy to unconsciously make Jesus into someone He's not. I find I constantly need to dismantle my default image of Him and see Him as He really is.

For, much to my surprise, it is not my own brain that knows best. Left to itself, my own brain will spin strange and elaborate misconceptions like a spider on steroids. My brain must focus on Scripture to get anything right.

So, back to our Scripture passage.

Back in Matthew chapter 11, Jesus responded to the false expectations of His buddy and cousin John the Baptist. He addressed as well the expectations of the miscellaneous Pharisees who were always hanging around, looking down their pointy noses at everyone else. He spoke about the cities that had rejected Him. Then He prayed (Matthew 11:25–27).

In His prayer, Jesus basically says, "Thank You, God, for hiding truth from the 'wise' and revealing it to children (i.e., those who don't think they have it all together)." He says that no one in fact can know God unless Jesus chooses to reveal Him to them. He says that all things have been handed over to Him.

Wait. This is an astonishing statement: the absolute power and sovereignty of God Himself, handed over—or *delivered*, in the original Greek—to a human being?

If you consider the scope of Jesus' teaching and the events that would later unfold, this context—Jesus establishing His authority—is central for the invitation that follows, and we often overlook it.

Later, Christ's resurrection from the dead would fully validate His claims to authority. After He finished His redemptive work on the cross, the Greek term applied to Him, *exousia*, denotes active power—the full ability to do as one wills . . . universal cosmic dominion not only of the physical universe, but the spiritual domain as well. Angels, demons, and all authorities and powers have been made subject to Him (1 Peter 3:21–22).

The Bible teaches that Jesus is God. He was with God from the beginning; by His power all things were created. When Jesus came to earth as a human being, He laid aside His divine majesty and took on the form of a servant. This One who was in fact the Lord of all the earth, the supreme Lawgiver, placed Himself under the Law so He could pay its debt on the cross and save those who come to Him. Jesus' resurrection, in fact, validates His authority and the fact that everything is in subjection to Him (Ephesians 1:22; Philippians 2:10, 11).

So if we look at the big picture here, Jesus was not just a funky street preacher or an all-around good moral teacher. He was someone far more radical. Jesus' absolute authority is the foundation of the commands He gives, like the Great Commission and everything else. This means that His invitation of Matthew chapter 11 is not just a fuzzy sentiment. He *will* deliver on His promise. It has real power and real, life-changing potential. It did for His hearers in first-century Palestine. It does for us today.

5

{Come, Ye Weary}

Come, ye weary, heavy laden,
Lost and ruined by the fall;
If you tarry till you're better,
You will never come at all.

I will arise and go to Jesus,
He will embrace me in His arms;
In the arms of my dear Savior,
O, there are ten thousand charms.

JOSEPH HART,
"Come, Ye Sinners, Poor and Wretched"

C*ome to Me, all you who are weary and burdened, and I will give you rest!*

How did Jesus say it? Was He whispering conspiratorially, smiling and kneeling down . . . or was He standing and shouting, His arms flung wide, palms outstretched, a precursor of His ultimate invitation on the cross?

We don't know.

We do know that His offer of rest would have struck a chord with His hearers.

In the Jewish culture of Jesus' day, the common people were tired. They worked hard, scraping together the means to feed themselves and their children. They saw much of their wages stolen by unscrupulous tax collectors.

I was recently among very poor people in a developing nation, and their condition reminded me of the situation of the common people 2,000 years ago. I saw how tired the people were—particularly the women—from doing the things that many of us take for granted.

They had no sanitary facilities in their splintered, tin-roofed shacks. No running water at all, let alone clean water their children could drink without danger of cholera or other diseases. They had to walk a mile to a pump, carrying plastic cans to transport the heavy, precious water back to their homes so they could drink, bathe, and wash their things. They had trouble finding fuel for their fires so they could cook their rice. They had trouble getting rice, for that matter. Their children were malnourished and often sick. There was no electricity at night. They lived in mud, with parasites, worms, and tarantulas. They dealt with unscrupulous officials, difficult medical care, and obstacles at every turn . . . just like the people of Jesus' day.

Interestingly, it seems that many people are weary in wealthier cultures today as well.

The people who study such things tell us that 70 percent of Americans don't get enough sleep. Before the invention of artificial light, most Americans slept ten hours a night. Now it's more like six hours; the mode is, "you snooze, you lose," and we are all trying to cram more into our twenty-four hours per day. So executives, medical students, mothers, teenagers, fathers—most of us—all whittle back on sleep hours in order to get everything else done.

Experts estimate that sleep deprivation and sleep disorders account for $100 billion in lost productivity, medical expenses, and property damage per year (we assume from sleepy people wrecking buildings or something). The National Highway Traffic Safety Administration estimates that drowsy driving accounts for 100,000 accidents each year, with billions of dollars in lost productivity and thousands of injuries and fatalities.

A while ago two commercial airliners landed at Reagan National Airport in my hometown without benefit of control tower clearance or guidance. Why? Because the air traffic supervisor was asleep. When the pilots couldn't raise this snoozing air traffic person by radio, they had to radio another control tower forty miles away and get controllers there to call the National Airport tower. *Ring-a-ling!* No answer. *Zzzzzzz.* Authorities relieved the controller of his duties; we assume he headed home and went straight to bed, poor guy.

Studies show that sleep-deprived rats become wasted, half-crazed, and eventually die. So what will become of us humans?

Well, rats don't go to Starbucks. In the United States, caffeine sales have soared in recent years, both in coffee as well as in the sales of energy drinks like Monster, 5-Hour Energy, Red Bull, Venom Death Adder, Jolt, Beaver Buzz, Bull Tonik, and Zombie Blood Energy Drink. Who thinks of all these names? And in spite of all the caffeine, people are falling asleep at the wheel, in business meetings, in church, in the control tower, and in the carpool line.

Record numbers are being diagnosed with narcolepsy, a neurological disorder that creates uncontrollable "sleep attacks" in which the patient zones out, dead asleep, at random moments. Years ago I interviewed a young man who'd been indicted for his role in a bank robbery. He told me his defense was that he had narcolepsy and was actually asleep at the time of the crime. Since my interview with him was conducted in prison, and he had quite a long sentence to serve, I don't think the narcolepsy defense went over very well with the judge.

A month ago two friends—a mom and her grown daughter—visited our home for the weekend. I'll call them Joy and Dani, which is appropriate, since those are their names. They shared the queen-sized bed in our guest room.

Now, though they are healthy and amazing people, Joy and Dani both happen to have sleep issues. They spent the first night at our house sleepwalking, shouting, and trying to save each other from a chandelier they were sure was falling from the ceiling in their room. (Please note that there is NO chandelier in our guest room.)

In the middle of the night we could hear Joy yelling, "Ohh-hhhhhhhhhhhhhhhhhhhh, noooooooooooooooooo!" followed by Dani shouting, "It's okay, Mom, I've got it!" as she waved her arms to protect her mother from the falling, nonexistent chandelier.

"Noooooooooooooo!"

"It's okay, Mom, I've got it!"

Over and over. Our family cowered upstairs, listening to the tumult and waiting for our poor exhausted friends to advance on us like zombies from *Night of the Living Dead.*

Teenagers are also notoriously sleep-deprived. Our high school twins are busy with academics, athletics, and complex social lives, not necessarily in that order. They get up at 5:30 in the morning . . . and then, between classes and sports, they spend almost twelve hours at school each day.

Last week I was driving my daughter and a friend home in the evening after track practice. They were talking about how tired they were, and the friend was saying how she was so happy because her algebra teacher had let her sleep in class that afternoon. If you know any teenagers, you know how they talk: "It was so like perfect cuz I just put my head down on my desk and slept like really well for like twenty minutes, and then I woke up at the very moment when the teacher was like talking about the very problem that I didn't understand! What are the chances of that? Like, yay!"

Anyway, it seems to me that everyone I know is tired.

But for us, just like the people of Jesus' day, the problem isn't physical exhaustion alone, difficult as that can be. Our weariness, whether we're poor or well off, goes deeper than that. People carry all kinds of burdens that cannot be eased by a few good nights of sleep.

Jesus wasn't saying, "Come to Me, all you who are tired, and I will give you My memory-foam mattress or My sleep-number bed so you can get some rest." No, the invitation is "Come to Me, all you who are *weary*."

The word that Jesus used for "weary" is *kopiao*, which means "to grow tired with burdens or grief." This is the kind of emotional fatigue that penetrates every pore in your body, no matter how much sleep you get.

I don't know what kind of burdens you may be carrying right now. It's worth taking a moment to think about this because many of us habitually carry heavy loads that press us way beyond physical weariness. The fact is, Jesus can take them right off our backs in a heartbeat.

6

{The Impossible Load}

Up this way, therefore, did burdened Christian run; but not without great difficulty, because of the load on his back. He ran thus till he came at a place somewhat ascending; and upon that place stood a Cross, and a little below, in the bottom, a sepulchre. So I saw in my dream, that just as Christian came up to the cross, his burden loosed from off his shoulders, and fell from off his back, and began to tumble; and so continued to do till it came to the mouth of the sepulchre, where it fell in, and I saw it no more. Then was Christian glad and lightsome, and said, with a merry heart, "He hath given me rest by his sorrow, and life by his death."

JOHN BUNYAN, *Pilgrim's Progress*

My guilt has overwhelmed me
like a burden too heavy to bear.
PSALM 38:4

There are so many weights and burdens in all our lives. It seems that they fall into four categories:

- The burden of *sin*
- The burden of *shame*
- The burden of *"shoulds"*
- And the burden of *suffering*

We'll look at the first three in the next few chapters and save the burden of suffering for later.

First, let's think about the burden of *sin*. This is the moral imperfection that just plain separates us from God. Earlier generations called His judgment of sin "damnation." It is no longer politically correct to use such language to talk about sin, though people use it all the time in its shortened version to talk about pretty much everything else.

The Bible says that everyone on the planet carries this load, and that we all fall short of absolute moral perfection and the glory of God. This burden is so heavy that it will kill us in the end unless it is removed, because the sentence for sin—a billion sins or one teeny-tiny sin—is the death of our souls.

There is no amount of good works that we can do that will somehow tip the scale and lighten our load. We cannot do enough penance to get rid of it. We can't pretend the load doesn't exist by distracting ourselves with pleasures. We can't effectively ease the pain of the load by self-medicating with drugs or alcohol or food or anything else.

Only Jesus can set us free from this impossible load.

Many years ago I saw a memorable movie called *The Mission*.

Maybe you saw it too. It is set in South America during the Spanish and Portuguese conquests there. Robert de Niro plays a slave trader named Mendoza. After the woman he loves rejects him in favor of his brother, he kills the brother in a sword fight.

Anguished and guilty, he joins the priesthood as penance and ends up being sent to a remote mission in the jungle with other Jesuits. We should note that the natives welcomed the first priest sent them by tying him to a wooden cross and sending him over an enormous waterfall to his death.

Mendoza has tied a huge bundle to himself. It is full of heavy, clatter-trap junk. It is his means of self-punishment and penance, and as he walks the long path and then ascends the towering cliffs that lead to the mission village, the pack on his back imperils his life. Yet he somehow staggers, exhausted, to the top.

There he slumps on the ground, covered in mud, tethered to his burden by heavy ropes. It's clear that this load will kill him, one way or another.

The natives—the very people he once hunted as a slave trader—stare at him. One approaches with a sharp, thick knife and holds it at Mendoza's neck. Mendoza bows his head in submission. He knows that his sins deserve only death.

Then the native takes the knife and slices through the thick cords that bind the burden to Mendoza's back. He pulls the enormous, dirty, clanking bag to the rim of the cliff . . . then kicks it over the edge. It falls and then splashes in the clean water and is borne away, over the thundering falls.

The native returns to Mendoza. The camera lingers on Mendoza's face as he slumps in a heap, overwhelmed by the absolute release of his burden and the forgiveness of the people he had once enslaved. He weeps, bowed over, and the native raises his head, stroking his cheek.

Mendoza weeps and weeps, and all the natives begin to laugh as they see the release of his inner demons. He begins to laugh too, through his tears. Others gather around, hugging him and rubbing his dirty head. He is free, relieved of the bonds and weights with which he was bound. It's like he's been born again.

This is a powerful picture of what Jesus calls us to. *He* is the one we have wronged, and He can forgive our sins. It sounds too good to be true. But if we bow our hearts and submit to Him, He can cut our stinking, heavy burden of sin's guilt and junk right off our weary backs and kick it over the cliff, *boom*, into His ocean of forgetfulness. Gone forever.

When God first called me, I was just a child. I was not a notorious slave trader or murderer. But as surely as Mendoza was doomed until his burden was removed, I was a soul in need of God's grace.

My mom was a believer. I'd heard the gospel from the time I could remember. One Sunday afternoon, I was sitting in our dining room. I remember the lace curtains, with sunlight shining through. I was looking at a wordless book, which had no words, only colored pages. It had been explained to me that the first page—the black one—represented my sin. The second was red, for the blood of Jesus that paid the penalty for my sin: death. The third was white, for the cleansing power of His blood. And the last page was shiny gold, representing the streets of heaven.

I was a small, earnest person. I wasn't aware of the huge load of damnation on my back, but I knew enough to know I was a sinner. I prayed right there to ask Jesus to forgive me, and I told Him I wanted to follow Him.

God called me to come to Him that day. I didn't hear any audible voice, and I was way too young to know very much. But by the power of the Holy Spirit, I bowed my head and came . . . and He took away the damning weight of my sin.

What's key here is that God doesn't just call us once, as if you come to faith in Him initially and then you're on your own.

Certainly at some point in our lives, yes, we come to Him in faith, and our names are written in the eternal Book of Life. We are born again, brought from spiritual death to life. Some of us may know a date and time; others of us might not be able to pinpoint just when that happened. No matter.

But just like our physical birth, our spiritual birth is only the beginning. It gets more interesting as we go along. Like a baby, we grow, learn to walk on our own, develop, and mature. Over the course of our lives, we come to Him again and again, as in my experience of "coming" to Him while walking on the beach during a time of weary turmoil.

As we'll see, coming repeatedly to Him is really a matter of sitting with Him, staying with Him, and remaining with Him over time. This being-a-Christian thing is a *relationship*, not just a belief system. So He continues to call, every day . . . *come to Me! Come, you who are weary, and burdened. Come!*

7

{Come Out of Your Bush!}

Sin has the devil for its father,
shame for its companion, and death for its wages.

THOMAS WATSON,
"The Ten Commandments" sermon

For those who do come to Jesus and find relief from sin and hell, we can still bear a more subtle burden. The burden of *shame*.

Right near the beginning of the Bible's great story, the first two humans lived in the Garden of Eden. It was Paradise. Literally. You know what happened. Satan, in the form of a snake—a subtle, crafty creature according to Genesis—tempted Eve to reconstruct her worldview and put herself in charge rather than God. Eve capitulated. So did Adam.

What was the result of their decision to eat the forbidden fruit? Nothing wonderful, despite Satan's promise that great things would happen. For starters, Adam and Eve experienced sin, separation from God, shame, and despair. They heard God walking in the garden in the cool of the day—a time they normally would have walked right with Him, naked as happy jaybirds, laughing, plucking sweet fruits and flowers, utterly enjoying the fragrance and friendship of Paradise.

But now it was ruined. Adam and Eve heard God coming and jumped into a bush.

Genesis says that the Lord God called to the man and said to him, "Where are you?"

God is God. He knew where Adam was. But He called to him, a call that echoes down through the centuries, calling to you and me.

"I heard you and I was afraid, because I was naked, and I hid," said Adam.

When I read that familiar story, tears sting the back of my eyelids. It's so sad . . . the pure delight and shimmering clarity of Paradise, botched and blotched by the smear of sin. Perfect intimacy, laughter, joy. Broken. And so Adam and Eve hid from the One who made them, loved them, knew them . . . and God Himself, walking in His garden, called them out of their thicket of shame and fear.

Come out, come out, wherever you are!

He calls still. He calls us out of the bushes, brambles, and thorns that can hedge us in. He calls us even though He knows right where we're hiding. *Come back to Me! Where are you?*

This is particularly poignant and powerful because many, many women who are earnest believers in Jesus still struggle with the issue of shame. Many carry shame over events that happened years earlier. Others carry dark secrets that no one knows. Many who carry heavy burdens of shame are super-productive, cheerful, and the first to volunteer to help someone else. No one would ever know the inner pain that haunts their thought lives. Others are psychologically crippled by shame that manifests itself in obvious ways like eating disorders, depression, and all kinds of dysfunction.

That's why Adam and Eve's story makes me cry. The pain of shame makes the power of the loving call all the more poignant. God called to them, "Come out!" He calls to me and you, whatever our story, "Come out!"

Maybe you've never come to Jesus. *Come!* Maybe you came to Him years ago, but you've been hiding and need to come back. *Come!* Come just as you are. Come out of that bush where you're hiding! Come out of your sin, shame, complacency, fear, anxiety, stress, self-harm, anger, pride, whatever it is that's holding you back! Don't wait till you're ready, or you'll never come. As the old hymn puts it, "If you tarry till you're better, you will never come at all."[1] Don't try to clean yourself up; you cannot do it. Wherever you are, even if you have a lovely life and everything is wonderful, hear the loving intimacy of Jesus' call.

Come!

Let's say it's a dark and stormy night. My backyard is squishy with wet dirt. My dog Gus is out there frolicking, dashing through flowerbeds and leaping from mud to mud. He's filthy. Pieces of mulch cling to his bedraggled fur, and his springy little feet are clotted with clay.

Do I leave my dog in the mud? Do I yell out into the night, "Gus, you may come inside once you've spiffed up and gotten yourself together"?

Well, no, I do not. Partially because the neighbors might think I'm strange. Or more strange than they already perceive me to be.

Even as a horribly imperfect human master, I know my dog *can't* clean himself. And regardless of that, I call him to come to the warmth and light of home, and he earnestly leaps and spatters his way toward me across the wet yard. I grab him at the door, get a towel, and kneel before my pooch . . . and in some sort of ancient foot-washing ceremony, clean him up.

Many of us are hindered by all kinds of mud and dirt. We can get stuck in burrs of repetitive sins. Maybe we've been sniffing around looking for love in all the wrong places. We can get stuck in habits of relying on our own strength. We can get spattered by patterns of pride, performance—more on that in a minute—and a critical spirit that just won't let up.

At any rate, we're tired. It's dark. We want to come back to the Light. But we think, *Oh, I'm too dirty. I need to clean myself up.*

But sorry, like my dog, we *can't* clean ourselves up.

Only the Master can do it, and He who so tenderly washed the actual feet of His clueless disciples 2,000 years ago will gently wash and refresh our souls today. All it takes on our part is the faith that He will take care of us and the earnest humility to come running to Him like a bounding puppy.

8

{The Burden of Shame}

Unless Christianity is wholly false,
the perception of ourselves which we have in moments of shame
must be the only true one.

C. S. LEWIS, *The Problem of Pain*

O kay," you say, "that sounds great. I want to be a bounding puppy, running freely by grace to my master. Love those dog analogies; keep 'em coming." But let's be practical. How can Jesus *really* clean us up and get rid of our shame?

I'm no psychologist, so what you should do is put this book down and go make a series of appointments for some pretty intensive biblically based therapy.

No, wait. Good counseling can be an incredible tool, but don't put the book down just yet.

What *is* shame?

It's a confusing emotion. Shame is, of course, intertwined with guilt, but guilt seems to be more connected with our actions, while shame has more to do with our identities.

If I do something wrong, I feel guilt and shame because my behavior has crossed a moral line. Guilt of this kind can be cleansed by confessing our sins to God, who really will forgive us our sins and cleanse us from all unrighteousness if we ask Him sincerely (see 1 John 1:9).

So if we feel this kind of guilt, it is a trigger: use it as a *stimulus for repentance.*

As you know, though, there is a deeper, trickier form of shame than the guilt associated with specific wrong actions. This deeper shame is more about *who we are* than *what we've done.* It shrinks and skews our personhood. It can make us feel inadequate, defective, defensive, and unworthy. Like guilt, this can come about through the unresolved effects of our own actions. Unlike guilt, though, this shame can also be the result of others' actions that have hurt and shaped us.

It can be the result of sexual, physical, or verbal abuse. It can come through violation and victimization, from crimes done against us by strangers or betrayal by people we knew and trusted. For years afterward it can be unconscious but constantly present.

Let me give you an example.

Just recently I remembered something that I've carried around for years, stuffed way down inside of me like a malignant tumor.

The memory came after I'd been talking with a friend who had come through some terrible struggles. The hard times had been helpful in a way though, because they had forced her to look at aspects of her life that she had suppressed for many years. She had been the victim of sexual abuse as a teenager, and the pain and shame of that violation had affected her ability, thirty years later, to really trust others and to have truly healthy relationships with the people she loved.

My friend and I talked a lot about what had happened to her as a teenager. Her story was on my mind . . . and then one day it stirred up something surprising for me.

I was in Washington, DC. It was a beautiful spring day, and I was walking on a cobblestone street in Georgetown. I went to graduate school there, and I love the historic homes, shops, and cafes of that part of the city. As I turned a corner, I looked down an alley . . . and then I suddenly saw what had happened to me in that very alley many years before.

I was in grad school, twenty-one years old. I was essentially living a double life. On one hand I knew that Christianity was absolutely true. On the other hand I was living as if it wasn't, and my behavior was like that of any random pagan on the street. I had been out with some friends. I'd had too much to drink. And in that very alley, late at night, I had been gang raped.

As I stared at that same alley in the daylight, decades later, my sudden memory of that awful night wasn't particularly clear. There weren't a whole lot of details. I didn't want details; it was painful enough to have the flashback as it was.

I knew that what happened to me was the perpetrators' fault. They bear responsibility for what they did. But I realized that even though I had repressed the memory, I had felt tons of guilt and shame for decades . . . guilt about the fact that I had been wandering away from God during that time in my life. God had tenderly wooed and carried me through the years since that appalling event. He had brought me back to a relationship with Him.

But now I could see how my experience of His grace had been affected by what happened. As a prodigal daughter whom God had called back to Himself, I had known I was forgiven for my sins, for the wrongdoing for which *I* was responsible.

But I had adopted a default "hiding" mentality. You would never have thought of me as a hider . . . I was happy, productive, loved being with people, and flossed regularly. I seemed just fine. But down deep, there was a whirling tide of worthlessness and shame within.

Now I realize that I had a tendency to lock off airtight compartments inside myself that I didn't reveal to anyone. After the alley memory, I saw how the residual effects of that dark night had long affected my ability to be naked and honest with Jesus and to expose my true self in my other relationships as well.

My experience is not unusual. Statistics are hard to gather, as many crimes are not reported, but it's said that every two minutes, someone in the United States is sexually assaulted. Some studies show that one in four women has experienced sexual abuse or assault of some type. Fifteen of sixteen rapists will never spend a day in jail.[1]

One psychologist says that shame is like a "vague, heavy cloud that determines your identity and never goes away. The behavior or external appearance of the person may or may not look good. However, inside the person is a big, empty hole. Intimate relationships between mates or parents and children begin to erode. Shame consumes the pleasant emotions."[2]

We can bear shame that has become so generalized and habitual in our thought life—a dull, pervasive feeling of worthlessness—that we don't even know its source. Shame is a feeling that manifests itself through behavior like the hiding mentality I've already mentioned. We hold off God and others at arm's length because we are afraid of truly being known.

Some who bear shame are well aware of it. Others may not even know it's inside of us. It may well be that the pervasive cloud of depression that hovers over us, or the driving personal dissatisfaction that roils within us, or the constant need to perform well for others—as we'll consider later—is actually the manifestation of shame inside.

The more I hear other women's stories and talk with them about the wounds in their lives, the more convinced I am that the burden of shame and the burden of the shoulds—anxious, performance-driven expectations of self—are more interrelated than many of us think they are. So let's park the burden of shame for a moment and move on to the burden of the shoulds. Then we'll consider Jesus' cure for both.

9

{The Burden of the Shoulds: Get Rid of Your Brontosaurus!}

If to-day he deigns to bless us
With a sense of pardon'd sin,
He to-morrow may distress us,
Make us feel the plague within,
All to make us
Sick of self, and fond of him.

CHARLES SPURGEON,
"Heavenly Love-Sickness!" sermon

"What are you laughing at?"
"At myself. My little puny self," said Phillipa.

RUMER GODDEN, *In This House of Brede*

The third kind of burden is the *shoulds*. It's a very heavy load. Like shame, it has to do with our self-image and how we feel about ourselves. So it's great news that we really do not have to carry this one either. We can lay it down.

Women are particularly subject to carrying around a huge pile of *I shoulds* on our backs. We stagger under the pressures of a performance mentality, comparisons with others, and all the other gross tonnage of religious and cultural expectations that we load on ourselves. "I should be thin"; "I should be as great a friend/wife/mom/sister/daughter/boss/whatever as so-and-so"; "I should be memorizing more Scripture and eating more vegetables and whole grains"; and basically, "I should be 'practically perfect in every way,' just like Mary Poppins." The list can go on and on, just about forever, and the weight of those boulders on our backs just gets heavier and heavier.

When I've traveled to rural parts of China, I've seen many women on the streets carrying impossibly heavy loads. They walk bent over with a long, thick wooden pole across their backs and huge baskets balanced on each end. They stoop beneath the weight as they carry heavy produce from the fields to the town market, miles away.

I once visited a little house church where the people met in a barn. The believers welcomed us in with steaming cups of tea, a few thin leaves floating in boiling water, and a large bowl of bright red persimmons. There was a big wooden yoke propped in the corner of the barn. Instead of baskets at either end, it had platforms; it was used to haul loads of short lumber.

Our host put the yoke on one of my friends. He was a big, strong American who worked out regularly. He staggered to his feet under the weight . . . and could not carry that heavy yoke, loaded with boards, more than a few feet.

Then the little pastor put on the yoke and carried it as if it was a minor encumbrance. My friend was a very good sport when our Chinese brothers and sisters in Christ all laughed at him. In Chinese. He was happy to provide the persecuted church a few moments of levity at his expense.

You see many elderly Chinese women in the streets, their faces weathered by years of work in the fields, their tiny frames hunched over, their backs bent from decades of labor. Now, as old women, they no longer have to carry those heavy yokes burdened with farm produce. But they have carried them for so long that now they *cannot* walk erect.

This can happen to all of us. Weighed down by psychological burdens we were never intended to bear—like the seemingly endless variations of "I should" performance thinking—we stagger under the load. Even when Jesus frees us, entrenched ways of thinking, living, and worrying have worn deeply rutted paths in our brains and loaded habitual tonnage on our shoulders. And so some of us walk bent over, eyes fixed on the ground, rather than erect and free, focused on the heavens above.

What are the performance burdens women carry today?

I emailed this question to various friends and within about two minutes received a ton of responses. Clearly this had touched a nerve.

"Women carry the burden of trying to 'do it all' and be good at it . . . but knowing we aren't," wrote one friend, the director of women's ministry at a huge, thriving church. She continued: "In small groups I've seen how women compare themselves with each other. They see the great things that others are doing, and add them to their 'shoulds/oughts' list . . . a public school mom sees the great places a homeschool mom takes her kids on field trips and realizes that she hasn't taken her kids to any of them!"

One mom shares about the mother/daughter weekend away where they talked about "becoming a woman," complete with James Dobson tapes . . . and the other silently berates herself for the birds-and-bees conversation she had with her daughter on a quick, random car ride home from who knows where.

Another friend just jotted a list of loads:

- the burden of living up to your mother's expectations . . . real or perceived
- legalism
- unforgiveness
- perfectionism
- judging

Another friend went crazy and put her inventory in the form of questions. These are all technically fears, because most of them are all based on a possible *future* outcome that may or may not happen . . . except for the last one, which may well be a present reality for some of us.

What if my kids don't turn out all right?

What if my husband doesn't love me anymore?

What if I'm not pretty/sexy enough?

What if I'm alone/single forever?

What if my parents don't approve?

What if I lose my job?

What if I'm stuck in this job?

What if I don't have enough money?

What if I can't lose the weight—and keep it off?

What if I can't take care of myself?

What if my health fails?

What if I lose my edge?

What if I'm not good enough/don't measure up?

What if I'm a coward and never step out to do great things?

What if the best time of my life is behind me?

What if this is all there is?

What if they see who I really am?

What if they find out what I did?

What if they find out about my past or my family?

What if I can't forgive?

What if nobody likes me?

What if nobody respects me?

What if I'm wrong?

What if I can't change?

What if everything I believe in is a lie?

What if global warming and war destroy the earth?

What if this really is the end of the world as we know it?

What if I never let God have full dominion over my life?

What if I don't have good hair?!

In many areas, there is the overwhelming burden of performance anxiety. You must do well in school so you can get into the right college and get into the right graduate school and get the right job offer. Some moms stress out about getting their toddlers into the right preschool in order to get a jump-start on this process. Others beat their brains out prepping their kids for SATs and other standardized tests. I know some women who are just about writing their kids' papers for them and calling them every day in college to make sure they're getting up for class. They are consumed by the world's standards of success, have turned into "helicopter parents," and seem terrified that unless they intervene and control their kids' performance, life as we know it will come to an end.

This is not a healthy thing.

Our public high school recently screened a documentary about the burdens students themselves feel in this exhausting environment. It's called *Race to Nowhere: The Dark Side of America's Achievement Culture*, and its description is just plain depressing: *"Race to Nowhere* points to the silent epidemic in our schools: cheating has become commonplace, students have become disengaged, stress-related illness, depression and burnout are rampant, and young people arrive at college and the workplace unprepared and uninspired."[1]

Meanwhile single women face all kinds of stress for a hundred different reasons. An unmarried friend told me how she stresses out about looming fears of losing her job and then possibly her home, as well as visions of being old and alone. And women in the workplace face huge pressures to excel, rise in the ranks, break through that glass ceiling that still exists, and get to the gym five times a week so they have toned calves and abs of steel. We're supposed to be feminine but tough, and if you are perceived to err too much one way or the other, it's easy to get shot down as a weenie or a witch.

Since I work at home, alone except for my faithful dog, I don't face those kinds of workplace pressures. So I instead stress about how unorganized my life is. I fantasize about a world in which every drawer is not a junk drawer—a happy realm where I can find the phone when it rings; where Tupperware tops and bottoms are married for life; where the garage actually houses cars and not old furniture, split bags of birdseed that mice are eating, and immense piles of too-small soccer cleats. I compare myself with friends whose spices are alphabetized and whose over-the-counter medications are not expired. I wonder why I found myself, the other day, distractedly watering an artificial plant.

I come into a cluttered room and cannot remember what I was looking for. I have to retrace my steps, as if my body can somehow recall what my brain cannot. I felt better the other day when a friend told me that she had taken her dog out for a walk, got down the street a block or two, and then realized she had forgotten the dog.

The other day I could not find my cell phone, so I used the landline to call it. (This is the only thing that I ever actually use the home phone for.) I heard the faint sound of my cell phone ringing somewhere downstairs . . . somewhere in the general area of the kitchen. I hunted it down like an audio bloodhound, circling, circling, and finally arrived at the refrigerator. I opened the refrigerator door, and there, sitting plaintively on a packet of ground beef, was my cell phone.

This is not unlike the time my friend lost her kitten and found it in the refrigerator eating out of the butter dish, but that is another story.

Meanwhile, in my burdened brain, I agonize over what to do with old Christmas cards I just cannot throw away, kids' old science fair projects that I seem to think will one day reveal the cure for cancer, all those cute little bottles of hotel shampoos that I really should take downtown and distribute to the homeless, and earrings that have no partner.

As it is, no one in my family has worn matched socks since 2004.

But let me clarify here. The performance mentality burden I'm talking about has to do with how we *feel* about ourselves, not the length of our to-do list. Sometimes I can feel plain old tired and overwhelmed by tasks, but that is different from measuring my self-worth and determining my identity according to how well I'm getting all my work done and whether I measure up to my own expectations and other people's perceived standards.

It is pretty clear that it's second nature for many women to carry all kinds of burdens that diminish their identity and freedom in Christ. If you boil it all down, these loads are basically big old packs of fears, performance anxiety, comparison with others, and cultural and religious expectations.

As I've said, some of the stuff on our backs can start out as noble, even biblical values. Are we teaching, discipling, mentoring, tithing, volunteering, and witnessing enough?

It's good to nurture others, to serve wherever we can, to seek to be a godly person, parent, spouse, employee, boss, sister, friend, and all those other roles we play. It's great to send thank-you notes on time, to volunteer in the church nursery and return our library books the same year we checked them out.

But in our busy world, it's dangerously easy to mix super-achiever cultural values into our journey with Jesus. We can end up downloading a string of tasks and activities into our faith to the point where it becomes a to-do list rather than a relationship. Even the good things can become weighty, clanking idols in our bags when they consume us and take our attention off Jesus. Some of them become so twisted and yet familiar that we don't want to give them up; they can become part of our identity, the image we work so hard to maintain. Even though it's so heavy, we wouldn't feel like ourselves without it.

Some of this may well come from our family of origin. Psychologists note that some families unconsciously set forth "shame-based" expectations.[2] This mind-set comes across through parents who constantly compare you with others. "Oh, I heard neighbor Susie has a 4.0! Sweetie, what was your GPA again?" There's a constant focus on performance so that the community, the church, and the office will think that the family is amazing.

I'm tempted to say that these are the families who write those annoying Christmas letters in which all their members are leading flawlessly productive lives, as in, Johnny just won the state's Perfect Boy Award, Janie was just admitted to medical school and she's only fifteen, and Mom and Dad just scaled Mount Everest without supplemental oxygen. But I would never say that because it wouldn't be nice. (For years I have wanted to send out fake Christmas letters in which our dog has been impounded for biting innocent toddlers and we are all in prison, having failed miserably and illegally at everything we have ever attempted, but that is rather dark and slightly passive-aggressive.)

In performance-based families, failure to achieve results in shame. There is a preoccupation with fault or blame. If something goes wrong or doesn't measure up, parents must find out who is responsible—so they can shame, blame, and isolate the offender in order to make sure such a travesty never ever happens again. These families thus train their children to be strong on head skills and weak on heart skills. Family members are good at critical analysis—rationalizing one's own behavior and figuring out who to blame—and clueless about how they really feel inside, because, after all, feelings are usually bad. What matters is how they appear to others.

Shame-based families look great on the outside. Inside there is little grace and a lot of unspoken rules. No one is allowed to notice or mention problems. So children are taught never to lie, but also understand that they can never say that Grandma's meatloaf tastes bad or that the neighbor boy hurt me. Family members communicate in code; you can't talk about real problems in a real way. There are elephants in every room.

Young couples certainly don't start out intending to raise their children in this kind of environment. But many husbands and wives unconsciously carry the hurts and dysfunctions of their past experiences right into their new homes. And eventually, when children come, before you know it, the habits of the shame cycle are carried on to a new generation.

Maybe that was your family. Maybe not. The great news is that we don't have to carry heavy loads of performance-based expectations. Sure, we'll always have a lot to do. But we can actually be free of all the blaming, fearful, comparing, despairing mind games that Satan loves to use to weigh us down.

Sometimes it takes a friend to come alongside and gently bring us to our senses and let us know that we don't have to carry such an awkward, unnecessary burden.

Imagine the conversation.

"Hi, what's that you're carrying? It looks so heavy."

"Who, me? What? Oh, oh, sorry, do you mean the dead, rotting brontosaurus I've got strapped on my back? No, no, it's nothing. No problem. I'm fine! Really! I've grown accustomed to carrying him; I've adjusted, and look, I still do so very much! It's fine. I've named him Harold."

No. We *can* be rid of our rotting brontosauruses. And please forgive me if you love someone named Harold. There are so many admirable Harolds in the world.

Have you ever carried something for so long that you cannot imagine living without it, like a dog that constantly worries his bone, over and over? Your burden can be relieved . . . and you don't have to walk hunched over, like the elderly women in rural China, as if you bore it still. Come to Jesus. I know, it sounds so backwoodsy fundamentalist, like all those movies in which the bad guy is some crazy preacher yelling at people to come to Jesus or else. But the real Jesus and His real invitation are much more compelling and tender.

You don't have to do well enough to somehow merit the invitation. You don't have to carry impossible loads and somehow perform as the ultimate achiever, getting everything right all the time. The Master does not expect us to be some sort of exotic performing circus dogs, wearing cute little hats and tutus and leaping through hoops of fire. He doesn't expect us to keep every rule and work, work, work all the time in order to feel okay about ourselves. The cycle of the shoulds is a burden He really can take away—if we are willing to let it go.

10

{Nakedness and Covering Up}

cov·er-up [kuhv-er-uhp]: *an attempt, whether successful or not, to conceal evidence of wrongdoing, error, incompetence or other embarrassing information. In passive cover-up, information is just not provided; in active cover-up, deception is used.*

Where did shame and the shoulds come from in the first place?

As we've said, shame made its appearance in the sin of our very first parents, Adam and Eve. Before they wrecked up (also known as the Fall), "the man and his wife were both naked and were *not ashamed*" (Genesis 2:25 ESV).

But once Adam and Eve decided to disobey God, "the eyes of both were opened, and they knew that they were naked" (Genesis 3:7 ESV). So they got busy and sewed some awkward fig-leaf outfits to cover themselves. Then they heard God coming and hid from Him.

Why did they then hide? If what Satan had told them was true, Adam and Eve wouldn't have felt ashamed. They would have been proud, confident, and secure in their newfound autonomy and anatomy. They could have reveled in their independence, feeling fine and free.

But Satan is a liar—back then and still today. He whispers lies to us all the time. Eve and Adam believed his lie. The result? Innocence ruined. Adam and Eve were literally dis-graced. They knew they were naked.

That had not been a problem before; but now they felt exposed, uncovered. They were afraid of God. Adam blamed Eve, Eve blamed the serpent, and ever since, shame and blame have been a constant theme in human beings' relationships with each other and with God. Shame came about as a direct result of sin; over the generations ever since, it has been passed down, a part of the human condition that will not be completely obliterated from our experience until we one day live with Jesus forever, when He will make all things new.

At the same time that the "evil twin" notion of "shame" entered human experience, the "good twin" notion of "shoulds" came in as well. These are different responses to the same root problem. The first thing our human parents did after they sinned was to desperately work hard to make some coverings for themselves so they wouldn't feel ashamed.

Sewing fig-leaf outfits doesn't seem so bad. Adam and Eve felt like they *should* have clothes on. So they got to work. But doing good work in our own human strength has been an inadequate cover-up since the Garden of Eden. (God made adequate garments of skins for Adam and Eve. Covering their nakedness required the death of an animal. This may well prefigure the system of animal sacrifices to pay for sin, which God instituted later, and the eventual, ultimate sacrificial death of Jesus Christ as atonement for sin.)

If we fast-forward from Eden to the first century AD, Jesus confronted the ultimate "should-ers" in His confrontations with the Pharisees.

The Pharisees held up impossible interpretations of Jewish law. They had codified the 613 commands found in the Old Testament and added the crushing weight of traditions that must be observed. Religious legalism on steroids.

For example, let's say you spit on the ground on the Sabbath, the day set aside in the week to refrain from work. The spit would make a furrow in the dry soil of the region, and so that would be considered farming . . . presto, you have broken the Sabbath.

Or the Old Testament law prohibited people from carrying things from a private domain—their home—to a public domain on the Sabbath. Since this inconvenient law could have prevented Jews from carrying cooked dishes to friends' homes for a Sabbath meal, the Pharisees ruled that adjacent houses linked by fences could become connected by a legal procedure creating a partnership . . . sort of a first-century homeowners' association. Presto, you could take potluck to the neighbors without breaking the Sabbath!

Jesus spoke often against this system that favored the few and manipulated the many. He called the Pharisees hypocrites because they focused on outward performance that people could see while ignoring inner character that only God could see.

Jesus was ready to love anyone who came across His path, including any religious person who was willing to chuck the pretense and come to Him. But He saw into the hearts of people who were unwilling and had no humility. No pliability. No care for anyone except themselves.

This was the key to the Pharisees' error. They were full of pride to the point that their hearts had become hard as rock. When Jesus healed weeping, needy people on the Sabbath, the Pharisees didn't care about the joy and deliverance of the human being in question. No, they were furious and indignant that Jesus would do "work" on the Sabbath and thus break the Jewish law.

In His visual way of getting to the heart of the matter, here's what Jesus said—among many other creative observations—about these guys.

Woe to you, teachers of the law and Pharisees, you hypocrites! You give a tenth of your spices—mint, dill and cumin.

But you have neglected the more important matters of the law—justice, mercy and faithfulness. You should have practiced the latter, without neglecting the former. You blind guides! You strain out a gnat but swallow a camel. (Matthew 23:23–24)

Jesus said that these fastidious spice-tithing, gnat-straining, camel-swallowing hypocrites heaped weights on the people. "For they bind heavy burdens and grievous to be borne, and lay them on men's shoulders; but they themselves will not move them with one of their fingers" (Matthew 23:4 WBT).

They had created a stifling atmosphere of works, duty, and expectations that had nothing to do with the heart of God. They were the "Should Police" who looked down on "sinners," people whose shame was nakedly obvious, like the adulterous woman whom they dragged out before Jesus while He was teaching a crowd in the Temple one morning.

They stood there in their nice robes, not at all naked. They made the woman stand right in front of Jesus. Trembling in her shame, probably just wrapped in a sheet or a shift, she was a lot closer to salvation than they were in all their finery.

"Teacher, this woman was caught in the act of adultery," they told Jesus. One cannot help but wonder if they'd set her up so they could catch her, or if they had just randomly been peeping in various windows like creepers, scouring the neighborhood for illicit activity. (And where was the man in question?)

"In the Law Moses commanded us to stone such women," they went on. "Now what do *You* say?"

Their question, of course, was a trap so they could have a basis to accuse Jesus of breaking the Law.

Jesus is so great. He didn't answer the babble of angry, self-righteous voices. Instead, He bent down and started to write on the ground with His finger. You can imagine that the woman is still standing before Him, but now He's kneeling down, perhaps at her feet.

They keep at Him. *Blah, blah, blah, blah! Blah!*

He straightens up. "Let any one of you who is without sin be the first to throw a stone at her."

Then He stoops down and writes some more on the ground. Was He writing their sins in the dust?

"At this," says the Bible, "those who heard began to go away one at a time, the older ones first, until only Jesus was left, with the woman still standing there.

"Jesus straightened up and asked her, 'Woman, where are they? Has no one condemned you?'

'No one, sir,' she said.

'Then neither do I condemn you,' Jesus declared. 'Go now and leave your life of sin'" (John 8:2–11).

I'm sure she did.

There were basically two kinds of people in Jesus' day.

Some were "sinners," indulging in sensuality, lust, paganism, and shamefulness. Like our nameless woman, caught in adultery. Figuratively speaking, they were naked in their sin, and Jesus died and rose again to clothe them in His righteousness.

And then there were the "religious people," the Pharisees. Figuratively speaking, they clothed themselves in layers of works and legalism, as if their own efforts would be enough to make them acceptable to God.

We may not be as obvious as the Pharisees, but many fall into the trap of legalism today. In some churches, particularly in other countries, there are many who feel that women shouldn't wear makeup or jewelry, or show their shoulders or their knees. You can't be a Christian and have a tattoo. You can't be a Christian and listen to certain kinds of music. There are all kinds of rules of what real Christians can and cannot do.

But "legalism" needn't be so obvious. As I've talked to women all over the United States, it seems that many struggle with more subtle expectations of what "real Christians" should be doing. Many measure themselves and one another by external efforts and works rather than truly *resting* in the grace of God. As I said earlier, we're caught in an endless round of performance anxiety, trying to do the right thing.

Going back to Adam and Eve for a moment, one can only imagine how prickly and unpleasant their fig clothes were. The principle is the same over the generations that followed: mere human efforts are so uncomfortable. They cannot make us feel okay about ourselves. It's difficult, useless, and endless work to try to clothe ourselves in the spiritual sense. Only when we admit our own nakedness and *need* for Him, every day, will God clothe us in *His* righteousness. Apart from Him, as Jesus put it in John 15, we can do nothing.

This is true of us even when we think we're dressed just fine, thank you. Even when we think that we have everything we need.

In Revelation, there was a church full of complacent, well-to-do believers who had lost their awareness of their spiritual need. Here was Jesus' message to those people:

> You say, I am rich, I have prospered, and I need nothing, not realizing that you are wretched, pitiable, poor, blind, and naked. I counsel you to buy from me gold refined by fire, so that you may be rich, and white garments so that you may clothe yourself and the shame of your nakedness may not be seen, and salve to anoint your eyes, so that you may see. Those whom I love, I reprove and discipline, so be zealous and repent." (Revelation 3:17–19 ESV)

We often hear the rest of this verse quoted as an invitation for nonbelievers to open their hearts to Jesus: "Here I am! I stand at the door and knock. If anyone hears my voice and opens the door, I will come in and eat with that person, and they with me" (Revelation 3:20).

But this was written to *believers*. They were nice churchpeople who had already come to Jesus. But they hadn't stayed with Him. They had come to Him by grace, and now they were fat and happy and had no needs . . . or so they thought. They didn't realize they had slipped to a place of spiritual nakedness and shame. They needed to come back to Jesus, fling open the door of their hearts, repent, and ask Him to clothe them.

Sometimes we need to do the same.

11

{The Shame Breaker}

Satan is ever seeking to inject that poison into our hearts to distrust God's goodness—especially in connection with his commandments. That is what really lies behind all evil, lusting and disobedience. A discontent with our position and portion, a craving from something which God has wisely held from us. Reject any suggestion that God is unduly severe with you. Resist with the utmost abhorrence anything that causes you to doubt God's love and his lovingkindness toward you. Allow nothing to make you question the Father's love for his child.

A. W. PINK, *Our Accountability to God*

Sometimes we study Scripture in little pieces, and that's good. But we need to constantly keep the whole enchilada in mind as well. If you look carefully at the macro picture of the Bible story, you can see the depth of what God really did for us. You can see how God actually deals the death blow to shame and to human efforts, works, and the shoulds.

As I've studied the biblical roots of shame, I've actually gotten excited about it. Not shame, of course. I've loved looking at the big-picture nature of God's plan, how He so tenderly deals with every single aspect of our need.

Here's a "greatest hits" look at the big biblical picture. It's important to trace this through the Scriptures, because it gives real weight to our understanding of how God's grace actually applies to us today . . . in our shame, in our shoulds, in everything in between. We need to base our hopes for healing on what is real, not how we feel. And this is real!

To the ancient Hebrew people, shame was a tangible, terrible, hideous concept. It came from total license and giving oneself over to dark forces. Shame was the lot of those who were unfaithful to God, idolaters, those who exalted themselves against God, who mocked righteousness, who trusted in earthly power and material strength. Pagan people who sacrificed their babies in their repulsive idols' fiery cauldrons were to be shamed. The ritual prostitution, beastiality, incest, and mutilations of Baal-worship's fertility rites were shameful, as was anything that caused a human being to degrade herself to the level of something less than human.

The very worst thing a Hebrew could wish upon an enemy was that he be clothed with shame, meaning that God's utter, abandoning judgment would rest visibly upon him. Job said to God, "Those who hate you will be clothed with shame" (Job 8:22 ESV). David wrote about the people who wanted to kill him, "Let them be clothed with shame" (Psalm 35:26 ESV), and "May my accusers be clothed with dishonor; may they be wrapped in their own shame as in a cloak!" (Psalm 109:29 ESV).

When the Israelites sinned against God, they too knew the disdain of real shame. You remember that early in their history, the people God had decided to call His own were in captivity in Egypt. They were Pharaoh's slaves, building pyramids and living in fear. God used a man named Moses to let them know that they were important to God and that He was going to do some pretty wild miracles to set them free.

After God has dramatically rescued the people from Pharaoh's army, Moses is up on Mount Sinai. He's in "God School," receiving the Ten Commandments and many other lengthy, explicit instructions about how these ordinary people whom God had chosen were to live in an entirely different way than the idol-worshiping, shame-full, hopeless people all around them.

Down in the valley, the people get tired of waiting for Moses. They are easily distracted and quick to conclude that Moses just isn't coming back. They feel they need a back-up plan. They petition Moses' second-in-command, Aaron, to make them an idol so they have something tangible to worship.

Incredibly, Aaron does so. He enterprisingly tells the people to give him their gold jewelry. Aaron gathers up all these bangles and jangles, melts and smelts them, and casts a golden calf.

I always wondered how big that calf was.

Scholars conservatively estimate that about three million people were part of the Exodus. Men and women alike wore golden earrings and nose rings too, kind of like today. So maybe Aaron melted down the earrings of, say, a million people . . . or a half million. However many they were, that's a lot of gold. I'm thinking Aaron probably was able to forge a good-sized calf.

Why a calf? At the time, among the locals, the calf was worshiped as a moon god; his upturned horns looked like a crescent moon. (Mature animals, by contrast, had their horns cut off.) According to some archaeologists, there may well have also been ancient Egyptian writings that referred to Pharaoh as a "Golden Calf," born of heaven, since Pharaoh was represented as the Sun King and Egyptian myths depicted the rising sun as a calf born of a heavenly sky goddess.[1]

So Aaron's choice of a calf was probably not because he was artistically challenged. ("Hey, guys, I can't make a giraffe or a hippopotamus. How about, you know, a *calf*?") No, the calf likely came from the Israelites' direct association with nearby pagan cultures, even Egypt, where they had just seen their invisible God do allegedly unforgettable miracles. But they wanted a God they could *see*, not some unseen deity who only dealt with Moses, who had gone missing anyway. So, following the pattern of the pagans around them, they got it going with a golden man-made image.

The Bible says that when Moses was coming down from Mount Sinai, he saw that "the people had broken loose (for Aaron had let them break loose, to the derision of their enemies)" (Exodus 32:25 esv).

Another version puts it, "And when Moses saw that the people were naked (for Aaron had made them *naked to their shame*, among their enemies)" (WBT).

Picture it: God had chosen the Israelites to be His people. He'd miraculously rescued them to be different from the world around them. They were to worship one God—not many idols— and live unpolluted lives. But as soon as their leader, Moses, was gone for a while, they went as crazy as a class of junior-high boys with a substitute teacher.

They "sat down to eat and drink and rose up to play," which basically means the whole scene got out of control, with naked dancing, wild promiscuity, and drunken stuff they would not want to remember the next morning. It was just like many a college fraternity party, with idol worship thrown in. And the neighboring tribes and peoples were laughing out loud not only at the stupid Israelites, but also at the God they supposedly belonged to.

At this point God could have abandoned His people to their well-earned shame and its effects. Forever. *Boom*. Annihilation.

But the story of the Old Testament unfolds in a stunning and counterintuitive way. Over the years, decades, and centuries, even though these people were forgetful, rebellious, stubborn, selfish, and often seem absolutely determined to make a shameful mess of their own lives, God rescues them. Tenderly.

As you read the story, you see that God has a plan in which, incredibly, the worst of the shame and its effects—isolation, separation, horror—will in fact fall one day upon *Himself*. His plan ensures that His people can escape the results of their stubbornness. *Rather than obliterating people for their sins, He will provide a means to obliterate their sin and shame.* And ours, right here in the twenty-first century.

I am dwelling on this because the issue of shame is not just a problem for a few people who've had certain tough experiences. Shame—tied as it is to sin and Satan—is in fact the key enemy Jesus came to defeat. It is the pervasive, malignant human illness He came to heal. It is the malevolent condition He came to cure. It is the hidden issue of many successful businessmen and super-achieving women.

Some people may seem like they don't suffer from shame at all. Perhaps it's buried very deep. Or perhaps some really don't feel shame because they've come from a wonderfully nourishing family and have had a healthier life-path than some of the rest of us. That is a great blessing. But the truth is that shame is in fact part of the inherited sin-nature that came from our first parents, passed down through the generations because of Adam's "federal headship," if you want to use the theological term. This inherited shame is a psychological cancer that will kill us if we don't put our trust in Jesus. The great news is that those who come to Him are saved from its deathly eternal effects.

Yet for many of us, saved from damnation, it can still cripple and crimp our lives, our witness, and our freedom in Christ. So we need to understand, *really*, how Jesus killed it at the cross.

The pattern throughout the Old Testament goes something like this: The people would come to God; they'd love Him for a little while. But then they'd get distracted and fall away. God was wounded—can you imagine the God of the universe allowing Himself to feel pain?—but He stuck with them. He'd allow them to absorb the consequences of their choices, then rescue and restore them. They'd be faithful, then they'd fall away because they had the attention span of gnats, and the cycle would repeat.

We are the same.

But over the thousands of years of this crazy story, God planted seeds of *redemption*.

Think of one of the Bible's most astounding pictures of this redeeming love, the story of Hosea. Briefly, what happens is that God tells one of His nice prophets to go marry a prostitute. He does, even though her name is Gomer. She wanders away from her husband, committing adultery over and over and over. Hosea tenderly woos her, loves her, and buys her back from her lifestyle of shame. He tends her wounds from those who didn't care about her, cleans her up, and restores her. It's an unforgettable picture of our radical unfaithfulness, rooted deep within us, and God's even more radical, redeeming love.

This is the same reason the prophet Isaiah wrote to the people:

> Do not be afraid; *you will not be put to shame.*
>   Do not fear disgrace; you will not be humiliated.
> *You will forget the shame of your youth*
>   and remember no more the reproach of your widowhood.
> *For your Maker is your husband—*
>   the LORD Almighty is his name—
> *the Holy One of Israel is your Redeemer;*
>   he is called the God of all the earth. (Isaiah 54:4–5)

and

Instead of your shame
   you will receive a double portion,
and *instead of disgrace*
   you will rejoice in your inheritance.
And so you will inherit a double portion in your land,
   and everlasting joy will be yours. (Isaiah 61:7–8)

Forgetting shame . . . receiving lavish blessings . . . it must have seemed too good to be true.

How could such a wonderful thing possibly happen?

12

{The Burden Breaker: Jesus Beats Sin, Shame, and the Shoulds}

He made Him who knew no sin
to be sin on our behalf,
so that we might become the righteousness of God in Him.

2 Corinthians 5:21 nasb

Fear is born of Satan,
and if we would only take time to think a moment
we would see that everything
Satan says is founded upon a falsehood.

A. B. Simpson, *Days of Heaven*

The wonderful thing did not happen any time soon, in human terms.

Seven hundred years after Isaiah wrote about deliverance from shame, the New Testament picks up this incredible theme with much more clarity. Quoting from Isaiah 28:16, the apostles Peter and Paul both recalled, "For in Scripture it says: 'See, I lay a stone in Zion, a chosen and precious cornerstone, and *the one who trusts in him will never be put to shame*'" (1 Peter 2:6; see Romans 9:32–33).

Peter and Paul and the New Testament guys could now see that, in fact, Jesus Christ—God's long-promised Messiah, the Cornerstone who was prophesied—was not just a fulfillment of the prophets' imagination. He was the actual, real Person who took the shame of sin upon His back . . . and broke it forever. Because of Jesus, there is hope.

> And *hope does not put us to shame*, because God's love has been poured out into our hearts through the Holy Spirit, who has been given to us. You see, at just the right time, when we were still powerless, Christ died for the ungodly. (Romans 5:5–6)

This is unbelievably good news, and not just because shame makes us feel bad and we want to feel good. The Bible intimates that everlasting shame awaits people who never confess their sin and admit their need for pardon. Part of the ultimate punishment of sin is horrific, unbounded shame, regret, and despair. Looking ahead to the final judgment, the prophet Daniel wrote, "But at that time your people—everyone whose name is found written in the book—will be delivered. Multitudes who sleep in the dust of the earth will awake: *some to everlasting life, others to shame and everlasting contempt"* (Daniel 12:1–2).

Shame entered the world when Satan brought sin into it; it will exit the world when sin is banished forever and everything is made new.

A judgment day is coming.

Some Christians today have abandoned their belief in hell in favor of alternative theologies that are more user-friendly. That's understandable; the very notion of hell is discomforting, horrible, and offensive. But I think it's hard to reconcile a disbelief in hell with the plain words of the Scriptures—particularly Jesus' pointed and frequent teachings on it—as well as the pictures of the End that are portrayed in Revelation.

> Anyone whose name was not found written in the book of life was thrown into the lake of fire. . . . Nothing impure will ever enter it, nor will anyone who does what is shameful or deceitful, but only those whose names are written in the Lamb's book of life. (Revelation 20:15; 21:27)

Followers of Christ have no reason to fear this definitive humiliation on that day of judgment. By His wild grace, we actually belong to God. Our names are written in His book. The ultimate shame we would have known as ungodly, unbought people has been removed by Christ's death on the cross. He says, "I will never blot out the name of that person from the book of life, but will acknowledge that name before my Father and his angels" (Revelation 3:5).

When I think about the burden of shame, what has helped me most is found in the beginning of Hebrews 12:

> Let us throw off everything that hinders and the sin that so easily entangles. And let us run with perseverance the race marked out for us, fixing our eyes on Jesus, the pioneer and perfecter of faith. *For the joy set before him he endured the cross, scorning its shame, and sat down at the right hand of the throne of God.* Consider him who endured such opposition from sinners, so that you will not grow weary and lose heart. (Hebrews 12:1–3)

The cross was, by design, the cruelest, most shameful sort of execution in the cruel ancient world. It was reserved for the lowest scum of the earth. It was public, pitiless, and painful. The horrific pictures we all have in our minds ever since we saw the film *The Passion of the Christ* film are historically accurate.

But Jesus endured the cross, says the writer of Hebrews, *scorning* its shame. The Greek word used for "scorn" in the text means literally to "think down," to despise, to hold in contempt. As Jesus was lifted up on the cross, you know that Satan was gloating, thinking that Jesus was pinned, the battle was over, and evil had won. The taunts, mockery, spit, blood, and shame of the cross were like a diabolical, gibbered frenzy of hatred vomited all over the body of Christ. Jesus hung there absolutely naked and exposed: the unclothed very picture of shame that our first parents had fled in the Garden.

Charles Spurgeon said:

Although our painters, for obvious reasons, cover Christ upon the cross, there he hung—the naked Saviour of a naked race. He who clothed the lilies had not wherewith to clothe himself . . . not so much as a rag to conceal his nakedness from a staring, gazing, mocking, hard-hearted crowd. He had made coats of skins for Adam and Eve when they were naked in the garden. . . . [Now] he himself, exposed to the pitiless storm of contempt, hath no cloak with which to cover his shame.[1]

But even in that seemingly helpless position, Jesus was still higher than the serpent. He looked *down* on the shame that was intended to reign over Him. He looked down at it with contempt. He was infinitely higher.

It is as if Satan had conjured a cup full of black poison, the cup of sin and separation from God. He watches in glee as Jesus drinks it down, every last drop of bitter, horrific shame.

Jesus dies. Every sadistic minion in hell thinks that it is finished, that the evil one has won.

And indeed it *is* finished.

But not the way that Satan wanted. Jesus was no victim. He was the willing, obedient Son of God. He drank down that dark goblet of sin and shame and flung it away, broken forever, blasted and cast aside like the big heavy stone that so ineffectively blocked His tomb.

He who knew no sin became sin for us; He who was clothed in righteousness became naked on our behalf. So, as Isaiah 61:10

says, we who were spiritually naked can now "greatly rejoice in the LORD; my soul shall exult in my God, for he has clothed me with the garments of salvation; he has covered me with the robe of righteousness" (ESV).

We were powerless to get rid of our burdens of sin and shame on our own. But as Romans 5:6–8 puts it, "You see, at just the right time, when we were still powerless, Christ died for the ungodly. . . . God demonstrates his own love for us in this: While we were still sinners, Christ died for us."

To put it in today-speak from a cultural rock star, U2's lead singer, Bono, has said this is the point of Jesus' sacrificial death. There are clear consequences to our sins. Christ took them on so we don't have to die. Our good words, no matter how good, just can't get us through the gates of heaven.[2]

So, back to the burden of shame and the weary inadequacies of human performance. Have these been completely removed, broken, and beaten on the cross?

Yes. Yes. Yes. And the more we revel in the Scriptures and actually soak in their truth, the more it will permeate our hearts and minds and eventually affect our experience.

But habitual ways of thinking and feeling can be quite stubborn. We can *know* truth and not *feel* it, and in this we must be patient. Perhaps many of us still struggle with remnants of shame in our experience today, for one reason or another. We'd like to have all that completely removed—*poof*—but perhaps it is still with us.

We may well carry some wounds until we reach eternity. Anyone who tells you that everyone will be completely healed now—

no more pain, the effects of every bad thing that ever happened expunged right now—is misguided. God can do that, of course. But for whatever mysterious reasons, He often does not . . . and so just as we do not become *wholly* sinless in this life, it may well be that some of us cannot be *wholly* free of shame or the tendency to perform in this life—this thirty or fifty or eighty or however many years that we live down here.

When we are tempted to dwell on it, however—when Satan would drag us into the tar pit of false guilt and shame—our rebuttal is ready. Jesus has paid its price. We will not suffer ultimate punishment of endless shame for sin. That penalty has been executed.

As Jesus said on the cross, "It is finished." The shame-debt is paid. Our names are no longer written in the annals of shame, but the grace-filled Book of Life. Done.

There's nothing we can add to this transaction in terms of our good works that will make it more effective or efficient. There's nothing we can take away from this transaction in terms of our bad works that will render it null and void. Again, it is finished.

The fact is, Satan loses.

And when we yet struggle with pesky or pervasive remnants of shame, here's a practical tool to help incorporate the reality of theological truth into our actual experience. It involves our brains. Not our intellect per se, but our squishy little brains themselves.

13

{How Your Squishy Little Brain Can Help You}

Therefore, I urge you, brothers and sisters,
in view of God's mercy, to offer your bodies as a living sacrifice,
holy and pleasing to God—this is your true and proper worship.
Do not conform to the pattern of this world,
but be transformed by the renewing of your mind.
Then you will be able to test and approve what God's will is—
his good, pleasing and perfect will.

ROMANS 12:1-2

metamorphó *(from* metá, *"change after being with," and* morphó, *changing form in keeping with inner reality") – properly, transformed after being with; transfigured.* Metamorphó *is the root of the English term "metamorphosis."*

Let's think about your brain. You carefully carry it around in your head with you at all times, and if you're like me, you probably don't think about it much. As I have contemplated this, I've been greatly helped by the writings of my friend Curt Thompson. Curt is a psychiatrist and a committed believer in Jesus. His book, *Anatomy of the Soul*, gave me a fresh understanding of the role of memory, particularly as it relates to events in our past that cause us to feel shame.

(I should boldly note that in my brief descriptions below, I am not doing justice to Curt's book. It is far better and more brilliant and scientifically sound than my few paragraphs about it. So feel free to get the book!)[1]

Anyway, back to your brain.

Within this meaty four-pound miracle of design are billions of little neurons. As you were saying to yourself just this morning, a neuron is "an electrically excitable cell that processes and transmits information by electrical and chemical signaling. Chemical signaling occurs via *synapses*, specialized connections with other cells. Neurons connect to each other to form networks."[2]

Psychologists have found that these little guys are communal in the sense that "neurons that fire together wire together." So neurons that repeatedly activate in a certain pattern are far more likely to continue to fire together.

As Curt Thompson says, think of your brain like a jungle. (This is not hard for me to do.) The first person who goes through the untamed undergrowth cuts a rough path with a machete. The second person to go through is unlikely to cut a whole new path; it's far easier to follow the slight path that has already been made, deepening and widening it as he goes along with his own machete. Others who follow will take that same path—why would they go to the extra work of deviating off the trail into dense jungle? And so the path becomes more and more clear-cut.

It's the same with our little neuron friends. When we remember something, we're firing neurons that have been fired before. The more frequently those patterns fire, the more easily they'll maintain that pattern in the future. So it's second nature to make the recipe you serve every week, while you have to look up the ingredients and instructions for the holiday dish you make once a year.

"We are often unaware of the depth to which memory contours our lives," says Thompson. "Understanding the ways memories are formed—and how memories, in fact, shape our present and future—can be a key to getting rid of shame."[3]

Scientists have identified various forms of memory.

First, we have implicit memory. Broadly speaking, this has to do with the brain's ability to recall things without conscious effort, as in, you don't have to think about how to drive a car, ride a bike, or walk across the room. At some point in your life you learned these things, and now your car-driving neurons all helpfully fire together so that the experience is automatic, so to speak, even if you're driving a manual transmission. This kind of implicit memory frees up space in our mental hard drive for other types of memory that need more conscious attention.

Implicit memory also has to do with nonverbal cues that run deep into our emotions in ways that are sometimes mystifying to us. For example, if your dad always sighed deeply when he was disappointed with you as a child, you may find that whenever your male boss sighs deeply, you begin to feel anxious and ashamed, thinking you're about to get in trouble or get fired . . . when in fact it may well be that your poor boss is just plain tired and his sighing has absolutely nothing to do with you.

Then there is explicit memory. This has to do with the recall of factual information, as in when someone asks you for your Social Security number or your mother's maiden name. It also has to do with the recall of autobiographical experiences over time, such as your memory of your vacation last summer or what you had for dinner last night.

These kinds of memories require deliberate attention—we have the sense that we are actively calling up an experience from the past. Thompson says that this feeling of remembering "enables you to tie moments together into a streaming progression that becomes the story of your life. Humans' ability to tell stories, which distinguishes us from all other living creatures, is a crucial part of how our minds connect us to God and others. Memory is the cornerstone of this undertaking." [4]

This is a profound point. If we are to truly connect with the story God is writing in our lives and how we are part of the big story He is writing in history, it's really helpful to think in these terms, even though they don't come naturally.

If we aren't aware of our implicit memories or their associations that can shape our behaviors today, we can encounter all kinds of mystifying conflict. Researchers estimate that in the emotional clashes between spouses, approximately 80 percent are rooted in events that predate the couple even *knowing* each other. [5]

So, to use the earlier example, if you had the Disappointed Sighing Dad, your husband's sighs might drive you right up the wall without you even knowing why. Or if your husband's mother lifted her eyebrows in a certain way when she didn't believe him as a teenager, he may think that your eyebrows-up facial expression means that you think he's lying . . . even though you may well just be paying attention to him with great interest.

Or, on a different level, let's say that your dad wore a certain kind of aftershave when you were young, and you loved climbing on his lap and cuddling there, enveloped in the scent of Old Spice or Polo or whatever. If you had a loving dad, that fragrance evokes a positive feeling every time you smell it. You may not even be aware of why you smile when some guy wearing that aftershave walks past you in a store.

But what if you were abused as a child, and your abuser wore a certain scent? Every time you encounter it as an adult, that smell would be indelibly linked with feelings of shame, violation, and pain—even if you did not consciously remember the abuse itself. You might subconsciously feel uncomfortable around men who smell that way, even though they are great guys.

There's a lot more we could say here, but here's the radical news, says Curt Thompson: you can actually change your *experience* of what you remember and so change your memory. You don't have to be a prisoner to memories-by-association and the feelings they stir up.

This may seem impossible, because many of us think of memories as absolute, distinct things that do not change. It's as if they are photos in an album or artifacts in a safety deposit box.

If you're like me, when you remember something, you view it as an exercise in fetching that particular memory, like pulling up a file on a computer.

But here's the wild thing: neurologists have discovered that memory is not like accessing an unchanging computer file that was created at a certain point in time years earlier. As far as our four-pound brains are concerned, there is no past or future. There is only *now*.

Of course actual events did take place in the past; time is real. But our little neurons and the hippocampus in our brains fire *in the moment*. So to remember your sixteenth birthday party is not to pull out an old file. Your brain, in this particular moment, fires and creates the memory in the present every single time you want to think about that particular event from the past.

This is revolutionary. It means that your past is not set in stone. (Again, of course, events from the past *actually happened* in real time. We're not suggesting some sort of denial or whimsical rewrite of the past.) You can change your *experience* of your past. You can change the way you *feel* about it.

As Curt Thompson says, "You have more power than you thought. . . . The manner and context in which you reflect on your story (in your mind) or tell your story (to others) become part of the fabric of the narrative itself. . . . The process of reflecting on and telling others your story, and the way you experience others hearing it, actually shapes the story and the very neural correlates, or networks, it represents."[6]

It's as if you cut a new path in your mental jungle. Rather than your thoughts going down the same old deeply rutted path as a million times before—that path of shame, blame, bad feelings, anxiety, whatever—you create a new path.

As you do so, consciously over time, your chummy neurons will fire together, once, twice, repeatedly . . . and eventually they will create a new pathway, creating a new experience for you.

Let's say that when you were a young girl and came home from school feeling sad, your mom comforted and affirmed you. Through repetition, your neurons associated sadness with a sense of comfort and trust.

But what if you came home from school feeling sad every once in a while, and your mom consistently made fun of you, told you to buck up, to be a big girl and get over it? You would associate feelings of sadness with feelings of shame and derision . . . and as you grew older you would avoid sadness at any cost because you could not stand those feelings of shame that came along with it. You would probably not even be consciously aware of this.

If you become aware of this association, however, you can break it by cutting fresh paths for your neurons. You don't have to get a little machete and whack away at your own brain. No, whether with a therapist or a good friend, you can discover and talk through the feelings your associations dredge up. You can reflect on God's immense affection that has nothing to do with performance and everything to do with total, crazy passion for YOU. You can put Scripture in your brain and purposefully reflect on it every time you feel sad. Bit by bit, you will be transformed by the renewing of your mind, and sadness will no longer elicit a companion feeling of shame, but comfort instead.

Here's something that has helped me.

As I told you earlier, though I first came to Jesus as a young girl, I wandered from my faith during parts of college and graduate school. It is hard for me to separate the shame I feel about things that happened to me during that season from my feelings of shame about having wandered away from the God who loved me and gave Himself for me.

So I have lots of shame triggers that pop up from the past. Some are large and some are small and ridiculous—stuff from yesterday or an hour ago. I once was talking with a counselor and mentioned that I often feel this little voice in my head that says, "You are so STUPID." I hear this when I remember various errors and sins from over the years or from last Tuesday. I was telling the counselor how I comforted myself with a picture of God saying to me, "Yes, honey, but you're *My* stupid!"

She looked at me, concerned, and said something like, "That's not normal." (I am probably remembering this wrong because I think counselors are trained precisely not to say things like that.)

Anyway, I digress. Given my new understanding of the brain jungle, the nature of memory, and cutting new neural pathways, I have found the following story quite helpful.

Earlier I described the joyful abandon with which we can come to Jesus, running like a bounding, mud-spattered puppy, if you will, to the Master who will tenderly clean us up. We'd be remiss, though, if we didn't think about the fact that we don't just come to Jesus. *He comes to us.*

He came to earth, to a specific country and region at a specific point in history. He lived among people just like us, with all the joys and frustrations of humanity. He took on limitations, pain, and sorrow. He had great friends who loved Him, and enemies who hated Him. He told stories, went to dinner parties, and, I am sure, laughed a lot.

One of his best-known stories that highlights the love of the God who comes to us is known as the "prodigal son," though it is mistitled. As pastor Tim Keller made so clear in his beautiful book a few years ago, *The Prodigal God*, the word doesn't mean "wayward," but rather, "recklessly extravagant." It means to spend until you have nothing left. We all know that the younger son did exactly that with his inheritance.

But the father in the story, who represents God, loves his messed-up son with wild, lavish, unconventional, extravagant love. When the young man staggers home from his pigpen, weak and covered in mud, what happens?

Jesus tells us that while the son "was still a long way off, his father saw him and was filled with compassion for him; he ran to his son, threw his arms around him and kissed him" (Luke 15:20).

In that ancient Near East culture, mature men did not run, especially well-to-do landowners. Prominent men did not hike up their robes and bare their legs to sprint.

But this father was watching and waiting for his son; he could not care less about cultural expectations.

God could not care less about the expectations of "religion," that only those who are dutiful, neat, and tidy deserve the attention of deity. No, He runs to us, gathers us up, and kisses us.

This is the glorious, actual reality of the kind of love God has for us. Even as He calls us to come, God the Father doesn't wait for us to limp and hobble all the way back to Him, His arms folded, shaking His head in disappointment because we've been so bad. He's been looking for us . . . just like He has looked for human beings ever since Adam and Eve. "Where are you?" He called to them. He calls to us the same . . . and runs with wild abandon to meet us where we are, even if we are "a long way off," like the son in the story.

So here's the deal: When I remember scenes that cause me shame, I consciously use them as a trigger, or stimulus, as I mentioned at the beginning of this chapter. I try to stop myself from bumping back down the deeply rutted path of the usual mental associations that Satan would just love to use to make me crazy. Instead, I use the stimulus to try to consciously think about a different picture. I think of the father in Jesus' story running toward the younger son, arms flung wide open, no matter what he'd done or how stupid he'd been.

If you're like me, that picture can change the focus. Instead of the story being all about us and our shame or our mile-long list of what we should be doing (which is where Satan would like to keep us), it's all about the Father and His love. It reminds me of the scene in *The Lion, the Witch and the Wardrobe* where there is a confrontation between Aslan, the great Christ-figure, and the evil White Witch.

The Witch says that because the boy, Edmund, has been a traitor, his punishment is death. Aslan agrees. But He will take Edmund's punishment upon himself and be killed in Edmund's place. Others who hear some of this are wondering what Edmund is feeling.

But, writes C. S. Lewis, *"Edmund had got past thinking about himself* after all he'd been through and after the talk he'd had [with Aslan] that morning. *He just went on looking at Aslan.* It didn't seem to matter what the Witch said."[7]

That is the picture for us. We can incorporate it into our brains to reroute our little neurons and teach ourselves truth. One way or another, we've all sinned against God. We've all been through a lot. But Jesus loves us, calls us, died for us. God welcomes us, running to us with open arms. As we keep looking at Him—intentionally fixing our eyes on Jesus—it won't matter so much, really, what Satan says to try to drag us back.

Looking at God, seeing Him more and more clearly as we are transformed by the literal renewing of our minds, we find that we don't feel shame so much anymore. We feel something else entirely. Amazement. Gratitude. And love.

Sit

{pay attention!}

14

{It's Epidemic: Spiritual ADD}

When I look back over the schedule I kept thirty or forty years ago, I am staggered by all the things we did. . . . Were all those engagements necessary? Was I as discerning as I might have been about which ones to take and which to turn down? I doubt it. Every day I was absent from my family is gone forever. . . . I would also spend more time in spiritual nurture, seeking to grow closer to God so I could become more like Christ. I would spend more time in prayer, not just for myself but for others. I would spend more time studying the Bible and meditating on its truth, not only for sermon preparation but to apply its message to my life. It is far too easy for someone in my position to read the Bible only with an eye on a future sermon, overlooking the message God has for me through its pages.

BILLY GRAHAM, *Just As I Am*

As you can see, coming to Jesus begins with an initial response to His invitation, His summons, His call.

We come, just as we are, and believe in Him.

But lots of people come to Jesus . . . and then, after a brief period of emotion, they wander away. Many return to the same old things that burdened them and held them captive before.

Jesus talked about that in a pretty frightening way when He was here on earth. We don't like to hear it today. Not too many popular preachers talk about this. But Jesus said, "Not everyone who says to me, 'Lord, Lord,' will enter the kingdom of heaven, but only the one who does the will of my Father who is in heaven. Many will say to me on that day, 'Lord, Lord, did we not prophesy in your name and in your name drive out demons and in your name perform many miracles?' Then I will tell them plainly, 'I never knew you. Away from me, you evildoers!'" (Matthew 7:21–23).

I don't believe that you can lose your salvation. But there are many who may well look like they know Jesus who in fact aren't known by Him. There are many who seem like they've come to Him—they do the right things and sing the worship songs and demonstrate emotion at the right times—whose hearts may be hard as stone and who have never truly received Him and become new people, born again of God. ("Yet to all who did receive him, to those who believed in his name, he gave the right to become children of God" [John 1:12]).

It's easy to walk forward in a flood of emotion, or to talk the talk of coming to God. But the actual reality of our coming to Him will evidence itself in the fruit of what happens when we *sit* and *stay* with Jesus . . . resulting in supernatural rest in Him, both now and in eternity.

As I said earlier, if you look at Jesus' teaching, you'll see the pattern. He tells people who come to Him to *sit* in a variety of ways. He told His followers to sit down and count the cost (see Luke 14:28) of following Him. He repeatedly told the crowds He taught and fed to "sit down" so they could listen to Him over time. We need to spend our time doing the same thing, studying and meditating on His Word. This cannot be hurried . . . and it is a distinctly countercultural choice in our speed-crazed, harried culture.

Sitting with Jesus requires the discipline of paying attention, fixing our focus on Him. We overcome our natural tendency—which is reinforced by the distracting, dysfunctional world around us—toward spiritual attention deficit disorder.

When we sit with Jesus, we learn who our Master really is. We learn who we really are. We sit down and actually gain our right mind. We sit with friends . . . whether it's in prayer, in worship, over coffee, under the weather, in tears, or laughing out loud . . . connected in communion and fellowshipping with others who have come to Jesus. And we actually prefigure our ultimate position in heaven, where Jesus is already seated at the right hand of God, His great work done, His reign secured. One day, says Scripture, we will sit and reign with Him forever.

But by way of introduction we must return to our metaphors from the world of dog commands—which I know you've been anxious to do.

Yes, yes, in the dog world, "SIT!" is crucial.

Canine trainers say that "sit" is the most important command your dog needs to learn. This is a reminder that you are in charge of things, not the dog. Trainers say to tell your puppy to sit before you feed him, before you play, before he goes out the door. This teaches the growing dog that he must respond to his master and that his own pleasures and desires are simply not the most important thing in his doggie life.

Our whoodle, Gus, is a little shaky in his Christian maturity . . . but even in his inadequate training on this front, I can see parallels to human spiritual development. When I tell Gus to sit, his eyes are always on me. His focus is single-mindedly fixed on his master, so he will see what I want him to do.

This is why this silly dog analogy is so important for you and me. We live in a land where spiritual ADD is absolutely rampant. If we don't intentionally, obediently fix our attention on Jesus, we will be distracted all day long, chasing our own tails and running after the dozens of squirrels that randomly skitter across our path.

I'm sure this is not a problem for you, but let me shyly share how this affects me.

Let's say it is a lovely morning, or even a dark and stormy morning, and I am sitting at my desk, reading Scripture. The computer in front of me is on, of course, just in case I want to research something I'm reading from the Old Testament.

Oops, there's a little *ping*. An email! Gee, it might be good news, or something exciting. Or maybe it's from Alistair Begg or Chuck Colson and it will incredibly resonate with the very Scripture I'm reading!

So I open the email. It is not from Alistair or Chuck, but from the noted Bible scholar L.L. Bean. Dr. Bean is having a helpful sale on outdoor wear. Hmmm, doesn't someone in our family need a jacket? I wonder what colors they have.

Oops!

I return to my Scripture passage.

Ping!

Wait, I obviously shouldn't open this new email. But I'm feeling a little tired now and maybe it will be something encouraging or rejuvenating.

Let's see, this email is from my good friends at Groupon. They're offering a special combo half-price deal for liposuction, tooth whitening, and carpet cleaning. Clearly this is a gift from God! I need all three.

Hmmm, I think, *what are "normal" prices for these services? I should research this.* I type "carpet cleaning" into my search engine, and look, here are today's headlines! *Wow, a man-eating saltwater crocodile was captured in the Philippines. Look at that picture! Who knew crocodiles could get so big? Hmmmm, don't I have a friend serving with a missions group in the Philippines? I know, I'll send her this picture with a funny caption. That will encourage her, which I know would be pleasing to God.*

God?

Oh right, I need to get back to the Scriptures.

I know, I know. I should turn the computer OFF or go climb a quiet tree and read my Bible while I'm out on a limb, which my spiritual life clearly is anyway. (Hmmm, is spiritual ADD what the prophet Jeremiah was referring to when he wrote to the Israelites, "I set watchmen over you, saying, 'Pay attention to the

sound of the trumpet!' But they said, 'We will not pay attention'"
[Jeremiah 6:17 ESV]?)

You get the picture. I'm not even a teenager; I'm a reasonably disciplined middle-aged person, and I can't even think straight when I have *one* seductive form of technology running. Add in the world of texting, phone calls, television, streaming movies, bits and bytes of constant connectivity, and smartphones, and you end up with stupid people.

You probably saw the recent book *Is the Internet Changing the Way You Think?* I haven't read it; I just thought, *Why, yes, it sure is* to myself and then went right on madly texting my son about how the lawn needs mowing this afternoon after school. Never mind that he is in high school psychology class, where he is not even supposed to have his phone turned on. Never mind that I'm supposed to be concentrating on reading God's Word. I just wanted to make sure that I texted him about the lawn before I forgot about it, which I will, of course, in about fifteen seconds because, after all, the Internet is changing the way I think.

Squirrel!

We most often think of children having attention deficit disorder, usually with some hyperactivity built in. This can affect learning, behavior, relationships, and everything else in a kid's life. More kids than ever before are being diagnosed with this disorder, and now there are more drugs than ever before to address the problem: Concerta, Aderol, Ritalin, and other methylphenidates.

Statistics show that increasing numbers of adults are also affected by ADD. They frequently find themselves unable to start or finish projects. They often underestimate the time it takes to complete a task, and after starting a task, overestimate the time left to finish it. This tendency is, of course, exacerbated by the pace and peculiarities of our world of constant connectivity.

I don't happen to suffer from this ailment; I have plenty of others. But I once took an ADD medication by mistake and was buzzed for hours, during which time I wrote thousands of words, cleaned my entire house, found a cure for cancer, and repainted the whole neighborhood—my heart pounding like a jackhammer the entire time. *Woo-hoo,* now I understand why that drug is so tightly regulated under the Controlled Substances Act.

Unsurprisingly, the book about the Internet says that cyber-space technology is affecting *everyone's* ability to focus and pay sustained attention to a thought or person or discourse.[1]

One reviewer noted, "Precisely because there are such vast stores of information on the Internet, the ability to carve out time for uninterrupted, concentrated thought may be the most important skill that one can hone."[2]

Those who are able to attend, to focus, will be the new literates—the people who possess a rare skill in high demand. Some futurists talk about a "survival of the focused," with those who are constantly distracted left far behind in the grand race of life.

More to our point, though, is this reflection: "I want to suggest that for those of us who are believers, [enhanced focus] is both foundational to and a byproduct of the practice of systematic Bible reading. My commitment to reading God's Word in a daily, rhythmic way carves out a space for concentrated thought, a harbor against the storms of information and activity that incessantly crash against my soul."[3]

Many of us have Bibles in various designs, colors, covers, and translations. Believers in persecuted countries would not believe the number of dusty, unread Bibles sitting on shelves in North American homes. And the most fundamental way for us to begin to know this One who has called us to come is to just plain sit down, grab hold of one of these Bibles, read God's Word, and prayerfully learn of Him. This is not sexy or appealing in our quick-time world that's hooked on speed—a culture that looks to faster and faster downloads and makeovers accomplished in the time it takes to watch a television show.

But sitting at Jesus' feet, so to speak, is the countercultural key to a deep, rich life of spiritual power . . . a soothing ancient secret that can change our experience of this wigged-out modern world.

15
{Be Still}

The Lord will fight for you; you need only to be still.

Exodus 14:14

He says, 'Be still, and know that I am God; I will be exalted among the nations, I will be exalted in the earth'.

PSALM 46:10

Do not strive in your own strength;
cast yourself at the feet of the Lord Jesus,
and wait upon Him in the sure confidence that
He is with you, and works in you.
Strive in prayer; let faith fill your heart—
so will you be strong in the Lord, and
in the power of His might.

ANDREW MURRAY, *The Prayer Life*

Sitting still is very hard for many of us.

A lot of people know a lot more about spiritual stillness than me. There are many detailed resources about the rich, ancient traditions of meditative, centering, "sitting" prayer that have characterized thoughtful believers for centuries. This book is not one of them.

All I know is that many of us need to *stop*. When was the last time you lay on your back on the floor before God, praying with your arms flung wide open, your body in the shape of a cross? When was the last time you knelt in your home, alone, and lifted your hands up before God? When was the last time you breathed deeply, parked your busy brain for a moment, and took your body for a walk, then sat outside and closed your eyes and let the sunlight sit on your face as you reveled in the holy love of God? Given the chance, our bodies themselves can actually refresh our relentless minds.

So many of us run around doing things all day, responding to various challenges, problems, and stimuli. We are constantly called upon to analyze situations. We use the wonderful brains God gave us. We think too much, talk too much, listen too little. But what fuels us, gives us wisdom, and soaks us in grace and peace so we can deal well with the crazy fray?

An intellectual understanding of God's Word and the information Scripture imparts is great. But it is not enough. We don't absorb who God really is in the same way that we learn algebra or history, so we can score well on our spiritual SATs.

All this must go deeper. We do well to stop and bring our hearts and bodies into the notion of being still. We need to figure out how, in the midst of our days, to sit at Jesus' feet. He's not physically here like He was for Mary and Martha and the early disciples. It may not be immediately apparent—which is how we like things—but He is here, and He can be known. We can learn of Him, not only absorbing His truths, but basking in His presence. It's like sitting with a great friend or mentor. Only part of what you enjoy and absorb from that person is transferred verbally. Much of the great comfort of friendship comes from simply *being* with the beloved one.

When Mary made the countercultural decision to sit with Jesus while her sister, Martha, made the default decision to run around preparing dinner, Mary wasn't just learning facts from Jesus. It was something more elemental and intrinsic: the transfer of personhood, enjoyment, and love that simply happens in relationships.

Joining ourselves to Jesus is far more mysterious than just agreeing to a contract, as great as that is. It's not like a military enlistment, though it is serious and intentional. It is more like a marriage covenant. There is a spiritual, mental, physical joining of everything we know of ourselves to Jesus, and unless we *sit* with Him, we'll find ourselves drifting away to other lovers.

If you're like me, it's easy to agree with the idea of sitting with Jesus, but it's hard to actually *do* it. Monday morning comes, and the temptation is always there to say, "I don't have time to sit! There's so much to do in my day ahead, so many challenges to be met! I need to go fast! And sitting isn't just going slow, it's actually *stopping!* If I stop I won't get anything done!"

That's rational. But God's principle here is pretty counterintuitive. It's also far more powerful than the logical human "wisdom" that says we must go fast in order to go far. I love Isaiah's prophecy in the Old Testament when God calls out to His people:

> This is what the Sovereign LORD, the Holy One of Israel, says:
> "In repentance and rest is your salvation,
>> in quietness and trust is your strength,
>> but you would have none of it.
> You said, 'No, we will flee on horses.'
>> Therefore you will flee!
> You said, 'We will ride off on swift horses.'
>> Therefore your pursuers will be swift!" (Isaiah 30:15–16)

At the time, in the late seventh century BC, Israel was threatened by an invasion from the celebrated king of the Assyrian empire, Sennacherib. He also wanted to snatch the ribs of the Egyptians, and so it was natural—humanly speaking—for the Jews to make an alliance with Egypt against their common enemy. Never mind that God had explicitly prohibited alliances with Israel's surrounding nations, particularly Egypt, their original oppressor from whom God had dramatically delivered them centuries earlier.

So God says to His people, *Repent, return to Me, rest in Me, and quietly trust in My strength for your deliverance. I am real!*

But the Israelites said, "No, no, thanks anyway; we'll just get away from the bad guys on fast mounts." At the time, Egypt, like Arabia, was famous for its champion horses.

Instead of relying on God's power—which had miraculously saved them in the past—the ancient Israelites put their trust in speed instead. Just like us. "No, God, we can't rely on You; it would take too long, and You might not come through for us, i.e., we don't really trust You. We'll just go fast, and that'll make us win."

The irony, of course, is that you can't win against the world by trusting in worldly means. As history sadly shows, Israel's swift horses didn't stop her from eventually falling to enemies who had superior military speed. Similarly, we can't outrun the world. We escape from the world's demands by slowing down, turning consciously to God, being still before Him, and trusting Him. Then see what happens.

As John Piper has said, God works for those who wait for Him: "If God is working for you, surely things will turn out better than they would if everyone else in the world were working for you, but not God."[1]

God's will is that we let *Him* save us, provide for us, fight for us. That takes real faith in the quiet reality of His presence, even when we don't see Him. Piper says that this kind of faith means three things when a tough situation arises: first we pray and seek God's counsel, quietly waiting to see what He wants.

Second, in prayer He'll sometimes tell us to literally be still, and so we "leave it all in His hands, trusting His supernatural involvement in the situation. I don't mean laziness or shirking of duty. I mean that when you are most prepared, most capable, most primed for battle and think that most hangs on you, He may say, 'Stay home, be quiet, pray and watch Me act.'"[2]

And third, says Piper, if the Lord says to take particular action, as in "'Prepare, train, work, fight, argue, struggle,' even then maintain that humble reliance on the Lord. Have a spirit of expectancy that though your labors are shabby, the final issue is the Lord's and He loves to work for people who wait for Him."[3]

Being still and waiting for God to lead is not a passive thing. It is active trust. That's why it's so hard, as we'll explore further when we turn a bit later to the burden of suffering. It would be a lot easier if we could apply a formula in every situation, as in, okay, I'll just wait for God to do a miracle every time. Or I'll just charge ahead and take care of this myself. Every time.

But our connection with Jesus can't be boiled down to formulas and rules. That's because it's a relationship, not a religion. With Jesus, we're giving ourselves over to a Person who is alive and dynamic. Not only that, but after He physically left the planet after His resurrection, He left us a Helper, a Comforter, an Advocate. The Holy Spirit can literally show each of us what to do in every single situation in our lives; He can show us whether it's time to jump on a fast horse or wait for a miracle.

Think about all the instances in Scripture when God told His people to do weird passive stuff and then He showed up, big-time, and did miracles to rescue them, like parting the Red Sea or causing their enemies to get confused and conveniently kill each other.

But there are plenty of times in Scripture where God's people sought His wisdom and He told them, *Hey, this is not a time to wait around; this is a time to act, and I will tell you what to do.*

For example, when God's people were getting ready to flee from Egypt, He told them to prepare a final meal. They were to slaughter a lamb and paint its blood over their doorways so the angel of death would pass them by. They were to eat and then leave, fast. No waiting around. No miracle that would halt Pharaoh just then. They needed to take their meal like this: "In this manner you shall eat it: with your belt fastened, your sandals on your feet, and your staff in your hand. And you shall eat it in haste. It is the Lord's Passover" (Exodus 12:11 ESV). Then they were to get out of Dodge, so to speak. In haste.

Similarly, when Jesus, God's Passover Lamb, was born, King Herod was like Pharaoh: viciously at odds with God's design. Herod was planning to kill all the baby boys in Bethlehem and the surrounding areas (Matthew 2). God knew this, and told Joseph, Jesus' earthly father, in a dream, "Get up!" *Get Mary and your child and haul out of there, son! Flee to Egypt. Stay there until I tell you, because Herod is going to search for the child to kill Him.*

And so Joseph did. He got up right away, in the night, and fled to Egypt. When Herod's soldiers so horribly slaughtered Bethlehem's baby boys, Jesus was safe.

Or think about the fascinating scene in Acts, when bad guys were determined to kill the apostle Paul soon after his conversion. They were watching the city gates in Damascus night and day, looking for Paul to leave so they could arrest him. Paul and his friends prayed and got the word from God that this was a time to take action. So Paul's disciples put him in a basket—I would have loved to have seen the great apostle of the early church stuffed into a basket like a load of laundry—and lowered him down the outside of the city wall so he could get away into the night, undetected.

So when challenges come, first, we wait. Be still, and know that He is God. Inquire of Him. Trust Him. Sometimes He will say, *Go, run, do something.* Sometimes He will say, *Wait. I will do something miraculous here.* The key for us, either way, is to inquire of Him and trust, rather than just jumping up and trusting in our own strength.

Sometimes challenges in life happen to teach us this very lesson. As the apostle Paul put it after his life had been threatened yet again while he was in Asia: "This happened that we might not rely on ourselves but on God, who raises the dead. He has delivered us from such a deadly peril, and he will deliver us again. On him we have set our hope that he will continue to deliver us" (2 Corinthians 1:9–10).

You know, often God can change our lives with just a few words, when we stop and truly focus on Him. I began this book by talking about how walking the beach and chewing on Matthew 11:28 changed my perspective and experience during a time of need. In fact, those hours of meditative reflection grew into the book you're reading now. That time of stillness yielded fruit that hopefully can bless others.

Similarly, author and pastor Louie Giglio says that he used to pray just one phrase every time he walked to his college classes years ago. For sixteen blocks he'd stride along, saying to himself, *I can't, but He can.*[4] Over and over and over.

Maybe other pedestrians dismissed him as a random, muttering crazy person, but this central truth of utter reliance on God—not our own willpower or abilities—has shaped Louie Giglio's passionate, Christ-centered ministry for decades.

There is no better cure for the confusion of the shoulds than to stop and fix our attention on God, not ourselves. *"Cease striving* and know that I am God,"* He says (Psalm 46:10 NASB).

In her book *The Scent of Water*, the early twentieth-century British writer Elizabeth Goudge gave me a prayer that I've loved for years. It's helped me to be still . . . and even though it's short, you just can't pray it quick. It's too rich for that.

Lord have mercy.
Into Thy hands.
Thee I adore.

Perhaps this might be useful in your own life. Get away from distractions; walk and mutter like a crazy person if need be. Take this prayer and think about each of these nine words. Reflect on how each phrase ties to Scripture. What *is* God's mercy? What's the nature of His redemption, forgiveness, and grace? Ponder what it means to put yourself in God's hands. Think about His hands, pierced for you. Put all you have, all you are, out there on the table for Him. Open up. Wait for Him. Listen. The unfolding glory of the truths of the first six words will, in fact, take you to the third phrase of adoration: a cascade of love and intimate gratitude whispered to the One who loves you more than you can know.

16

{Sitting in the Hurricane}

"My heart is fixed! O God, my heart is fixed! I will sing and give praise." After being with Jesus, half the questions that trouble you will be answered and the other half will not seem worth the asking. . . . You are His beloved, and your heart rests in that blessed fact.

CHARLES SPURGEON,
"The Christ-Given Rest" sermon

I'm not suggesting that we all drop out of the world and move to a commune in Vermont. All the communes there are already taken anyway, mostly by people from Ben & Jerry's.

I *am* saying that we can rely on God, not on how fast or efficient or multitaskingly talented we are. He can equip us to get everything done in each day that is His will for that day. "Sitting" with Him is a way to demonstrate that we trust Him. It is a choice of faith.

I don't have a prescription of *how* to sit with Jesus. I'm just waving the flag, like a yellow flag at the Indianapolis 500, to say, *Whoa, caution! Other people have wrecked, and you will too unless you slow down!* In fact, better still, I'm waving the red flag: stop for a while. Then you can rejoin the race. Stop. Sit with Jesus. The Holy Spirit will show you how.

A few weeks ago I was in the Dominican Republic on a trip with our church. This trip is an annual high school outreach to people in very poor neighborhoods near Santo Domingo, and so 278 students and adults went there to bring the gospel and physical help to the poor, in Jesus' name. We were like a small town descending on the island to help other small towns, with a dozen different outreaches from construction to medical aid to feeding hungry people to evangelism to discipleship.

There are many stories to tell from this trip—do you know how big the tarantulas are in the Dominican Republic?—but suffice it to say that during our time there, Tropical Storm Emily developed in the sea somewhere, and she was mad. She concentrated her winds, rain, flooding, and fury on the DR. When we looked at online weather maps of the corkscrewed storm heading our way, we could see that the Weather Channel had thoughtfully labeled the very center of the hurricane's major impact like this: "McLean Bible Church missions trip."

Not really. But that's how it felt.

Now, this wasn't a big deal. We were staying in a secure hotel that had backup generators and plenty of food and water. What we could not comprehend, though, was how our Dominican friends living in shacks in the mud could make it through the storm.

We were able to work with them in the rain for a while, but then we were told that for safety's sake we had to get the students back to the hotel, which would be on lockdown and high alert. Crazy inches of water fell every hour. The winds picked up.

Thankfully, Emily didn't develop into the monster hurricane that the weather models predicted. The damage was nowhere near the catastrophe that many had feared. We were grateful. But we were frustrated . . . what was God thinking? Here we were, all of us charged up and ready to go out and do great things for His Kingdom, stymied by the wind and the waves, which we thought He controlled. So what's up with that?

But here's the point: during the time that we were sequestered at the hotel, our youth group staff decided to lead a half-day seminar for the high school students on "how to study your Bible." Figuring they had a captive audience, they weren't going to waste the time. We had been having worship services and great biblical teaching . . . but we wanted to take this opportunity to remind kids how they need to be able to *stop* and *sit* when they got back home to their normal schedules. They need to connect with Jesus. And what better investment for teenagers who want to *do* missions than to teach them how real missions is fueled: by going out in Jesus' power, not our own?

The next day, when the skies had partially cleared, we were able to return to the Dominican neighborhoods. Because of flooding, we had to improvise. Many of us ministered in areas that weren't even on the radar screen of our original plans.

For example, my son Walker ended up talking with members of one of the San Francisco Giants' affiliate baseball teams, who were lodged at a field facility in the DR. They couldn't practice because of the floods on the fields, but they were there, just waiting for something to happen. And here came the Jesus team, so to speak, fresh from sitting with Him. Walker and some of our other colleagues ended up leading a bunch of these young baseball players to Christ.

Interesting.

Maybe there's something to be said for stopping, sitting, and drawing close to Jesus. God's plans are bigger and more wondrously strange than what we might imagine.

That's a great lesson for teenagers. Adults need the same.

Maybe we won't be grounded by a hurricane, which is pretty much what it would take to get many of us to stop. But we need the practical reminder to sit down, turn everything else off, and fix our attention on Jesus. We need to get back to basics.

This is absolutely countercultural, and there is no fancy, high-tech way to bypass it. Even if we read our Bible on an iPad or a smartphone or whatever, we have to sit still and take it in. We have to go slow. We hate that; North Americans, especially, like *fast*. But it is healthy to make the decision to slow down and learn of God. In order for its person to grow, the human brain and body actually need to sometimes attend to Just One Thing.

The Gospels repeatedly mention how Jesus would remove Himself from busyness. His days were full of meeting poignant human needs . . . but then He'd withdraw to a quiet place, away from the crowds, or even to "a desolate place" . . . why? Because no one else would be there. I know this has been said before, but if you're like me, we don't need new truth here; we need to attend to the great old truth: If Jesus Himself needed to get away from distractions to pray, how much more do we?

Sometimes He would beat His brains out in ministry. Sometimes He would skip whole towns. He was in step with the Spirit, and knew when to go fast and when to stop.

Do we think that our generation of shallow multitaskers somehow doesn't need the ancient spiritual disciplines of prayer, reading the Word, and meditation? These cannot be hurried, and we cheapen our lives and our understanding of Jesus when we pretend they can. Some mornings I'll be in a hurry and say to myself, *Oh, I'll just read what Charles Spurgeon or C. S. Lewis or some classical theologian says about this passage in the Bible.* That is nice, particularly since those are great resources and not from some silly person who has no clue.

But the ancient way, the best way, is to sit down and soak our souls in prayer and in the Scripture itself. We must be still to hear the still, small voice of God's Holy Spirit, who alone can truly illuminate the Word of God for us. This is how we gain wisdom. This is how we can be people who actually have something strong and true to offer the needy world around us. This is how we build our lives on the Rock that can't be shaken, no matter how great the power of the hurricane around us.

17

{"Learn from Me"}

Christianity, if false, is of no importance,
and if true, of infinite importance.
The only thing it cannot be is moderately important.

C. S. LEWIS, *God in the Dock*

As we sit and digest the Bible in prayer and meditation, we discover more and more who God *really* is. Otherwise we will run around with an image of God that is actually just a figment of our own imaginations. Learn from Me, He says. Learn who I really am.

I've already mentioned that many of us who've grown up in the church may have two-dimensional Sunday school pictures and skewed assumptions in our heads, like Wimpy Jesus or Distant Angry God. Jesus is far more strong, grace-full and startling than we assume. Our human tendency is always to reduce Jesus to a manageable size or to make the Father and the Son conform to pictures in our minds. And it can be hard to have any kind of picture of the Holy Spirit, mysterious as He is. We have to guard against this, lest the triune God become a caricature and we lose the wonder and power of this mysterious grace and Person.

Additionally, in today's environment, if we have a small, self-oriented view of God, we can use Him as a weapon or a means to judge others, as if we have the corner on truth. We end up becoming very poor representations of the gospel in the process. Truth is sharp and clear . . . but sometimes our minds and motives are fuzzy. When that happens, God becomes like an NFL franchise in the culture wars and we insidiously begin to use Him—*our* brand of Him, wearing *our* team colors—for political means, to win arguments, to divide and judge people, or just to move our particular ball of interest down the field.

There's much we could say here, but the great danger for many of us today is simply to have a general, false view of God that suits our tastes . . . otherwise known as Salad Bar God.

Salad Bar God is the result when we, as consumers, consider various ideas about the Almighty and pick and choose just what we want. Reaching under the sneeze shield, we take a pinch from the Scriptures, a scoop from what sounds good on the airwaves, a little from our experience, and a helping of moving stories we've heard from others. We skip the things about Him that we don't much like—the things that might give us gas or make us uncomfortable in some other way or that are hard to swallow. We put our God Salad together just how we want. To paraphrase the old Burger King ad, "Have Him YOUR way!"

Salad Bar God is, of course, different for every person. I was on a trip to the Middle East and one of our guides was a sharp young Israeli I'll call Omer. We talked about faith, and he told me that he didn't care for Christianity or Judaism. He'd thought about it all and had made up his own interpretation of God.

"I call it Omerism," he said. "It's a religion of one."

Omerism or Oprahism or Ellenism or you-ism fits right into our individualistic culture in North America. Everyone just needs to find his or her own "truth"—which is an illogical contradiction of the very meaning of "truth"—and everyone's a winner. And just like a soccer league for small children, all gods get trophies for participating, no matter how bad they are.

Another, more sinister concoction that one can put together in the salad bar of ideas in this post-9/11 world is the Politicized Fundamentalist Terrorist God. I'm not speaking here about Islam but about how some members of the media seem to love to paint even halfway sensible Bible-believers as intolerant, dangerous, crazed extremists . . . and some Christians seem to bring on this label, assuming that God will move just now according to the judgments they deem appropriate. So natural disasters get blamed on immorality; manmade disasters on the same. Maybe there is a cause-and-effect in some of these cases. Maybe not. Do we know?

There's another picture of the Almighty that some people put together. It's out there lurking in the guilt-laden subconscious of millions of Americans. I've met many who struggle with this picture of deity. We'll just call him Mad God, and He simply doesn't like anyone who went to Catholic school. He only likes mean nuns from the 1950s and '60s.

Most adults suffering from Mad God Syndrome are wonderful people who tiptoe about avoiding Him and hoping He won't notice them.

One of the most abhorrent versions of God that lots of consumers in America like very much is Rich, Benevolent Uncle God. This is the twenty-first-century spin on the prosperity gospel that's been around for decades.

I don't need to assemble a bunch of egregious teachings or quotes here as examples of my point. You know this stuff when you see it. Usually it sounds something like this, though often in nicer and more subtle words: If you come to Jesus, He will bless you . . . not only spiritually but *materially*. Come to Jesus and you'll have a nice house and a good job and you'll hopefully drive around in a neat little BMW or a big ol' Mercedes SUV. Come to Jesus and He'll cure your cancer. You just need to have enough faith that He will do what you want. And then, if you have some problem and God doesn't intervene and save you from death, well, maybe you didn't have enough faith.

Did the apostle Paul or Peter or Stephen or the saints of the early church or Dietrich Bonhoeffer, Maximilian Kolbe, the ten Boom family, Bob Ziemer, Betty Olsen, Yesu Dasu, Justiniano Quicana—or millions more martyrs you may or may not have heard of, beloved of God—not have enough faith?

As John Piper says, we are exporting this prosperity gospel garbage from America to the poor around the world. "Come to Jesus," well-meaning people assure poor villagers, "and your pigs won't die and your wife won't have a miscarriage!"

To return to my metaphor, of course human nature wants only the sweet, easy-to-digest parts of the salad bar. But the gospel isn't about assembling just what we want and like. The gospel is a declaration, a meal, a feast. Take it all or take none. It is either true . . . or false. If it's false, please, let's reject it and make up our own truth. Much easier.

But if it's true, let's take it all—even the parts we don't like or can't quite digest just now. God has made a feast that will nourish us for eternity . . . but we must take it all on His terms, not our own preferences. We accept it because it is true, not because we think it's all just yummy.

Out in the cacophony of salad bar culture, there are plenty of other false images of God, such as Irrelevant God, Grandpa God, Transgender God, Global Warming God, Buy Gold Now God, Cut Taxes God, Raise Taxes God, Nonexistent God, and Dead God . . . but these assumptions about the Almighty's existence or lack thereof are not germane to our discussion.

If only we could put God in a box.

The point of all this is just a simple reminder. If we are people who've truly come to Jesus, the next step—for the rest of our lives—is to sit down, take time, soak in the Scriptures, and feed ourselves the strong Word of God. We need to know what we believe and why we believe it. We need to be able to give a coherent reason for belief, as well as a personal story.

Having said that, it's not as if we can master some sort of airtight apologetics that will dazzle the world with the truth of the gospel. Neither God's existence nor His full character can be *proved*. None of us is going to argue anyone into the kingdom anyway.

But God's reality *can* be deduced by those with eyes to see and ears to hear. Our job is to be like detectives documenting the chain of evidence in a case that leads to a logical conclusion. We can follow the trail of clues about the reality of God and the nature of His truth and lay it out for our friends and colleagues to consider.

A lot of people today really like Jesus and respect Him as a great moral teacher, prophet, and good guy. But any talk about Jesus that ignores His assertions of deity, His sinless life, His unbiased love, and His real remedy for human sin by His bloody death and resurrection, is not really talk about Jesus at all.

There's a passage from C. S. Lewis that is so often quoted because it is so precisely true. Lewis says that people often say they're ready to accept Jesus as a great moral teacher, but not His claim of divinity. Yet:

> A man who was merely a man and said the sort of things Jesus said would not be a great moral teacher. He would

either be a lunatic—on the level with the man who says he is a poached egg—or else he would be the Devil of Hell.

You must make your choice. Either this man was, and is, the Son of God: or else a madman or something worse. You can shut Him up for a fool, you can spit at Him and kill Him as a demon; or you can fall at His feet and call Him Lord and God. But let us not come with any patronizing nonsense about His being a great human teacher. He has not left that open to us. He did not intend to.[1]

Wow. This Jesus business is on *His* terms, not ours.

18

{Sit Down and Count the Cost}

Is it a sense of your load which makes you say you are not able? But consider that this is not a work, but a rest. Would a man plead, I am so heavy laden that I cannot consent to part with my burden; so weary that I am not able either to stand still or lie down, but must force myself further? The greatness of your burden, so far from being an objection, is the very reason why you should instantly come to Christ, for he alone is able to release you.

JOHN NEWTON,
The Works of the Rev. John Newton

If you're a dog person, you know that our furry friends have a habit of getting absolutely obsessed with less-than-delightful things. One time our most famous dog, Lewis the Giant Labradoodle, came bounding toward me with joy. I saw dirt on his big white snout; he had been digging in the backyard.

He proudly dropped his treasure on the deck; it hit with the distinctive thud caused only by rigor mortis. Yes: it was a very long-dead squirrel. I had the hardest time convincing Lewis that this was not a desirable thing to carry around with such love and pride.

Perhaps your dog is obsessed with dead fish, like Smokey the Dog of my husband's youth. Whenever the Vaughns would vacation at the beach, Smokey would find any dead fish—or crab, sand shark, jellyfish, whatever—that had washed up on the shore and would gleefully wallow in it. Side to side, on her back, legs up in the air: roll, roll, roll.

For some dogs, the deep affection is not for something dead, but for an item that smells almost as bad. A well-gummed, slobbery tennis ball. Teenaged boys' socks. Dirty underwear fished from family members' laundry baskets.

The usual dog command for such situations is this: "LEAVE IT!"

Here's a human story that shows the same idea.

A few years ago an experienced twenty-seven-year-old outdoorsman named Aron Ralston went out on a solitary day hike in a Utah canyon. He neglected to tell anyone where he was going.

As he was climbing up through a narrow gorge, a stone above him—about the size of a bus tire—shifted and fell toward him.

He instinctively threw both arms up to protect his head. The 800-pound boulder, tumbling toward him in what seemed like slow motion, crushed his right arm against the rock face on the side of the gully and crashed to a stop.

Aron was alive, incredibly, but trapped as surely as a bear in a trap, his arm pinned between the unmovable boulder and the unyielding rock face.

You probably know Aron's story. His book became an international bestseller and an acclaimed movie called *127 Hours*. He survived for more than five days in the remote canyon, pinned in place. He pushed, twisted, turned, and tried everything he could think of to escape. He rationed the contents of his backpack and water supply. He thought of family and friends. Then, knowing he was nearing the end, he scratched his own epitaph on the side of the rock wall.

His trapped arm was actually decomposing. Gangrene had set in. *It is poisoning my body. I don't want it,* he thought. *It's garbage.*[1]

He had tried to cut off his arm and free himself earlier, but his dull pocketknife could not saw through bone. But now, in a near-death epiphany, he suddenly realized that if he torqued his arm far enough, he could *break* the bones in his forearm and then he could cut around the shattered pieces. It would be like bending a two-by-four held in a table vise; he could bow the whole arm until it snapped in two.

He had some medical training, so he sort of knew what he was doing, even in his weakened state. He figured out the angle, arched his body just right, and torqued his arm with all his might to exert the maximum downward force on his radius bone.

A crack like a gunshot reverberated through the empty canyon; the bone fractured. He did it again, this time focusing on his ulna. Another crack, and now both bones were broken.

Aron took his dull pocket knife, figured out where to cut, and began sawing away on the part of his arm he could access. He severed skin, tendons, arteries, muscles, nerves. Agony: but better than death. He cut, sawed, twisted, and tore for almost an hour . . . and then the last shred of flesh ripped free.

"A crystalline moment shatters, and the world is a different place," Aron said later. "Where there was confinement, now there is release . . . my mind [is] surfing on euphoria. As I stare at the wall where not twelve hours ago I etched [my epitaph], a voice shouts in my head: 'I AM FREE!'"

Aron rigged bandages, stumbled out of the canyon, and eventually made his way to civilization, medical attention, and his anxious family and friends. His story is disturbing, gutsy, inspirational . . . and I could barely read it without cringing at the thought of it all.

I know nothing about Aron Ralston's spiritual state. But his story gives us a graphic picture of a profound spiritual truth.

You probably know the New Testament story of the rich young man who came to Jesus one day and knelt in front of Him.

"Good Teacher," he said, "what must I do to inherit eternal life?"

This man was moral, wealthy, respectful, respected by others. He had it all . . . but knew enough to realize he needed something more.

Jesus said to him, "You know the commandments, right? Do

not murder, do not commit adultery, do not steal, do not bear false witness, do not defraud, honor your father and mother . . . you know all that, right, son?"

The guy was eager and earnest. "Yes, yes, I've kept all these laws from my youth." You can imagine him smiling, hopeful, thinking, *I can do this, I can get in!*

The account in the Gospel of Mark says that Jesus looked at the guy "and loved him." It was like He saw into this young man's soul . . . and He discerned the one thing that was trapping him, the thing that had him pinned, the force that was holding him back from real joy and real life.

"You lack one thing," Jesus said. "Go, sell all that you have, and give to the poor, and you will have treasure in heaven; and come, follow Me!"

Jesus knew that once the young man got rid of his stuff, he could come to Jesus, free and unencumbered.

But the man's face fell. He went away, grieving . . . "for he had great possessions" (Mark 10:17–22 ESV).

Sometimes this story scares the wadding out of us because we think it means we all have to sell all our possessions in order to follow Jesus. So we ignore it. But as Tim Keller points out, this encounter is the only recorded instance of Jesus saying such a thing to a would-be follower. The point wasn't a blanket prohibition on wealth. The point wasn't the fact that this man was financially well-off. The point was that Jesus penetrated like a laser right to his very heart and incinerated his expectations about faith.

The young man had been thinking that religion was something he could add to his life to make it better. People are still like this today. We think, *Ah, Christianity will make my life run more smoothly, kind of like a program that will boost capacity and speed on my computer hard drive.*

But an encounter with the *real* Jesus revolutionizes everything. He takes us completely apart and then puts us back together in a new way. And He will always discern the one thing that holds us back.

The rich young man thought he was doing a fine job keeping the Old Testament commandments. But he was managing to ignore the very first one: "You shall have no other gods before me" (Exodus 20:3).

His possessions had become an idol. Jesus will always discern our idol: the thing that we love, depend on, trust in more than Him. It could be a human relationship, prestige, power, money, self-reliance. It could be drugs, alcohol, food, sex, or exercise. It could be political ideologies, love of country, or a religious view of God that has nothing to do with who He really is.

Jesus looks at each of us. He loves us. He says, "I see it. I see that one thing: it's the malignancy that's killing you."

To continue to borrow from Tim Keller's sermon on the rich young ruler,[2] he cites an article that appeared in the *Village Voice.* Exploring statistics that showed that the number of people engaging in unsafe sex was going up, in spite of health warnings and tons of sex education, the author then revealed that he had done the same. In spite of ample knowledge of the risks, he continued to indulge in anonymous, dangerous sexual encounters. "I recoiled so much from what I had done that it seemed to be not my choice at all. *A mystery,* I thought. *A monster did it.*"[3]

We all have our monsters. Most of us hide them well, but they can make us do the very thing that will kill us. The rich young ruler was the epitome of a respectable, moral person. He didn't look monstrous. But Jesus penetrated to his heart, and He saw the ugly idol there.

Jesus had a habit of repelling would-be followers. If He had wanted to build a megachurch, He went about things in all the wrong ways. His branding and PR were off. He didn't design a user-friendly way for people to come to Him; He made things hard rather than easy.

No one wants a hard message. We want life to be comfortable, growth and blessing to be free, and our challenges to be like eggs, over easy. We're like the people of Isaiah's day, who said to the troublesome old prophet, *Hey, don't harass us with a difficult message; no,* "speak to us smooth things, prophesy illusions!" (Isaiah 30:10 ESV).

But as Charles Spurgeon has said, "Jesus was too wise to pride Himself on the number of His converts. He cared rather for quality over quantity." [4] At one point in the Gospel of Luke, great crowds were following Jesus wherever He went . . . until He turned and challenged them with a few deal-killers, like if you come to Me and don't hate your own family, and even your own life, you can't be My disciple.

It sounds incredibly harsh. But again, the idea here is that Christ isn't an add-on; He's not a Jesus app you stick on your smartphone and access when you feel like it or when you're sick. He comes first. He will revolutionize everything in your life.

Jesus was clear: "For which of you, desiring to build a tower, does not first sit down and count the cost, whether he has enough to complete it? . . . So therefore, any one of you who does not renounce all that he has cannot be my disciple" (Luke 14:28, 33 ESV).

This is so different from our own day. Many churches and pastors and teachers seem to gauge their identity and sense of success by the number of their adherents. Many soften the message of the gospel so hearers won't feel like it might cost them too much to come.

Jesus wasn't interested in building crowds; He was building His church. He knew how fickle and divided people were. He knew, near the end of His life here on earth, that the cheering crowds would follow Him one week, throwing down their coats and waving palm branches, shouting things like "Hosanna! Yay! Jesus for President! Love You!" and then a few days later hired crowds would yell, "Crucify Him! Crucify Him!"

So what do we do?

The key is in the second part of the story about the rich young ruler. Jesus tells His disciples that it's easier for a camel—the biggest land animal they were familiar with—to pass through the eye of a needle than for a rich person to enter the Kingdom of God.

The guys are understandably depressed. "Then who can be saved?" they moan.

Here's the kicker. Jesus says, "With man it is impossible, but not with God. For all things are possible with God" (Mark 10:27 ESV).

Yes, it's impossible, humanly speaking, for any of us to rid ourselves of our idols. Nor can we free another person from spiritual bondage. "No human being can liberate another human being from the enslaving power of the love of money," says John Piper.[5] Or the love of anything else.

It's one thing if you're lying in a gutter with a heroin needle stuck in your arm. Most of our slavery isn't so obvious. For many of us, it's our comforts or the "good life" itself that is choking us from a rich, free life in Christ. We think, *I can do Jesus and still hold on to lesser gods, like money and education and position and other culturally acceptable idols.* Many of us haven't had to count the cost—so we live safe, unradical lives as a result.

We can't give up our idols on our own. They are too entrenched . . . and Satan, the enemy of our souls, does not want us to be free.

The enemy always wants us to say no to God's call, or more often, *"Later. I'll do it later. I'll come later."*

But there's hope for us too! Jesus is stronger; He can do what is impossible. All that is necessary on our part is *willingness.* It's the simple acknowledgment, *yes.* "Yes, Lord, I am willing. I can't, but You can. Yes, Lord, this thing inside me that makes me feel good or loved or significant or powerful is, in fact, a monster. It's killing me."

In Aron Ralston's case, it was obvious that he was going to die unless he got rid of his arm. For the rich young man who came to Jesus, his danger wasn't so obvious: he looked like he had it all together. He was wealthy, moral, respected. But he wasn't willing to cut out the very thing that was going to kill his *soul.*

What's holding you back, really? Whatever the idol, let it go. In the glories of heaven one day, no one will mourn what he or she left behind to come running to God. Such things will be like broken toys, dead squirrels, rotten fish, or a monster that was going to kill you.

Of course, there's an alternative: Have it your way. Don't come.

19
{Sit Down and Gain Your Right Mind}

"Something is wrong when our lives make sense to unbelievers."

FRANCIS CHAN, *Crazy Love*

Jesus looked at the young ruler and loved him. His heart stirred for the men and women He met—not just those who had a lot and needed to leave something behind in order to come to Him, but also for the ones who had nothing.

Like the naked, bleeding, crazy guy Jesus met one day while out on a little sailing trip with His friends.

Jesus and His disciples had sailed from the Jewish side of the Sea of Galilee to a region inhabited by Gerasenes, or Gadarenes. These people were culturally more Greek than Semitic, which accounts for the pigs that play a starring role in the story.

The disciples and Jesus bring the boat from the shallow waters up to the rocky shore. They hear horrific, stomach-turning screaming. The locals know that there's a crazy man who lives up in the hills. He has "an unclean spirit." He roams around among the tombs and caves screaming and cutting himself with sharp stones. Even when people had mustered the courage to try to bind him so he couldn't hurt himself or others, he had broken the shackles and chains they put on him. He has superhuman, inexplicable strength.

I visited that place a few years ago. The lake is lower than it was in Jesus' day, but the land is much the same. I could see the scene in my mind: Jesus' boat is drawing toward the rocky shore. The hill is steep and covered with thick yellow weeds. He and His friends hear the screaming first. Then they see this wrecked shell of a human being—a thing festering with destruction and hatred—running down the hill, shrieking and gibbering and foaming. Blood runs down his naked body as he shakes and shouts at Jesus. He's no longer a recognizable human being made in the image of God, but more like something taken over, bent, controlled, running straight toward Christ.

Jesus gets out of the boat, advancing like a liberator toward the man.

The disciples are frozen in place. This is not of earth. It is a confrontation between the breath of heaven and the stench of hell.

The evil presence inside this poor man screams out to Jesus. It would kill the disciples if it could. It is stronger than these humans. But it knows who Jesus is, and Jesus is stronger still.

"What have You to do with me, Jesus, Son of the Most High God?" it yowls.

Jesus actually talks with this thing, telling it to come out of the man, asking its name.

"Legion," it shrieks, "for we are many."

Meanwhile a huge herd of swine are grazing on the side of the hill.

"Send us into the pigs!" the demons beg Jesus.

He does.

The unclean spirits spew out of the man and into the pigs. The entire herd, about 2,000 animals, suddenly starts shaking, snorting, rolling, and squealing in a frenzy of confusion. Then they rush down the steep hill, trampling the weeds with their mud-caked hooves, and into the lake. Within just a few minutes of churning chaos, they are all dead.

The men herding the pigs run into the nearby town. When the townspeople rush to the scene to see what in the world is going on, they find the man who had been demon possessed now "sitting there, dressed and in his right mind" (Mark 5:15).

The disciples or Jesus must have given the man some of their own clothes, gently cleaned him up, and bound his wounds. But the local people didn't seem to care that the demoniac has been helped and healed. They were used to the old dark powers, and had even accommodated them. They were used to their way of life and livelihood . . . and now, by the way, their main source of income was gone, drowned in a lake of floating bacon.

And they were afraid.

They begged Jesus to leave them.

As Jesus departed, the man He healed asked if he could come too. No, said Jesus. "Go home to your friends and tell them how much the Lord has done for you, and how He has had mercy on you."

The man went on to do so in the surrounding areas . . . "and everyone marveled." You bet they did. People could see that meeting Jesus had changed him forever.

What was his new name? He had been Legion, of course, for the many evil spirits inside of him. A Roman legion was made up of 6,000 men.

We don't know what Jesus may have renamed him. Jesus had a tendency to give His friends nicknames. Maybe He called him Un-Legion or One or Beloved or Friend. Or Fred. All we know is that instead of roaming and wandering—a rampaging creature who could find no rest—he was sitting, clothed and in his right mind, after his encounter with Jesus.

Ahhh! That's what Jesus does!

I wrote earlier in this book about how He clothes our nakedness. Our sin and shame are forgiven and cleansed because He took our shame upon the cross. Mr. Legion crosses Jesus' path before the cross . . . but he too is saved by grace and clothed by the gentle mercy of God.

Maybe you can't really relate to this story. Its elements of demonic possession and suicidal pigs are just too strange. But the fact is, even the most far-gone, desperate, weird, and awful situations can come to calmness and closure in Jesus. The restless brutality and self-destruction of a man who had lost his mind could be relieved. The one who had no place to go could come to Jesus. The one who had been utterly restless could sit and rest.

It's rare to come across people today who are naked and living in cemeteries. What's not so unusual is to come across people who are hurting themselves. Whether because of post-traumatic stress disorders, mental difficulties, abuse, or fragmentation, many struggle with dark troubles. Some may seem just fine on the outside, but inside they don't feel at all in their right mind.

For example, there's a virtual epidemic today of people who feel so much emotional pain that they resort to terrible ways to release it. Like Legion, they cut themselves.

Experts estimate that about 4 percent of the population practice self-injury. Studies of high school and college students, however, put the number at approximately one in five. My friend who works with university students counsels kids who cut quite frequently. You'd be surprised how prevalent it is in church youth groups. According to one young woman, "People who haven't cut can't understand how it can make you feel better . . . but it does.

. . . You feel like you are going to explode and you don't know what to do with the emotional pain. When you cut, there is a kind of release or freedom in it. Then, it's like an emotional high. You release all this pain that had been building. Like any addiction, it's a coping mechanism."[1]

I have a beautiful young friend who struggled with self-harm for years. She's in college now. Her body will be marked for as long as she lives in this life with the evidence of her pain and torment. Series of scars that look like hash marks are all over her arms and legs. She was a high-functioning teenager; much of her anguish was hidden. She wasn't running around shrieking like Legion, bound by steel chains. But she was bound all the same, restless and unable to stop hurting herself. Satan, who prowls around us all, seeking to control and destroy, had her in his grip. But just as in Legion's day, Jesus is stronger than the Dark One. Christ broke through my friend's pain, and she came to Him and found rest for her soul.

"I used to try to hide my scars," she says. "I was ashamed of them. But now they remind me of what I've been saved from. So now I see these scars as marks of grace."

Whether people are cutting themselves up externally or constantly cutting themselves down internally, Jesus really can break through. He can take away the spirit of destruction and calm the restless heart. He can save us from hurting ourselves. He can restore our minds . . . and change our stories forever.

20

{Sit with Friends}

Is any pleasure on earth as great
as a circle of Christian friends by a good fire?

C. S. LEWIS, *Letters of C. S. Lewis*

If you want to go fast, go alone.
If you want to go far, go together.

AFRICAN PROVERB

The great thing is that we don't just sit down with Jesus. When we come to Him, we also connect with a new family. We sit down with friends.

Before he met Jesus, sat down, and gained his right mind, Legion had been solitary and shunned, his only encounters with people being when they fled from him or came in mobs to chain and shackle him.

Afterward and forever, Mr. Legion was part of a community, the family of God.

Every person Jesus healed, He restored to community. Some had friends already, as Legion did before he lost his mind. Or the guy whose buddies lowered him through the ceiling so Jesus could heal him. Some had only their fellow outcasts, like the ten lepers Jesus healed. Once they were cured, however, they could be restored to the larger community of the healthy and no longer be considered unclean.

But many were alone. Think of Mary Magdalene, from whom Jesus cast out a bunch of raving demons. She was probably not a very popular person in the neighborhood. But after her connection with Jesus, she became a key figure in the early community of Christ-followers. Or Zacchaeus, the most hated tax collector in town, who met Jesus, had a party, and started giving his wealth away. You know he ended up with all kinds of friends.

Or think of Saul before his conversion. He was a Pharisee, so presumably he had a group . . . though they don't sound like a very fun gang to hang out with. But after Saul came to faith in Christ, he immediately became part of a wonderful community. Ananais, who only knew Saul by his murderous former reputation, called him "Brother Saul" right from the beginning. Saul got a new name—Paul—and new friends with whom he lived, laughed, wept, and worked for the rest of his life. When friends from the church at Ephesus knew he was sailing away to his eventual death, they crowded around him on the beach.

"When Paul had finished speaking, he knelt down with all of them and prayed. They all wept as they embraced him and kissed him. What grieved them most was his statement that they would never see his face again. Then they accompanied him to the ship" (Acts 20:36–38). This would never have happened with proud, judgmental, pre-conversion Saul, who was probably just about the most unkissable man on the planet.

In today's Facebook world, "friend" has become a verb. So you friend someone by clicking on a little request button online . . . and as a result you can end up with thousands of friends, most of whom you would not recognize if they actually came to your home and rang your doorbell.

I do like the idea of "friending," though. It *should* be a verb, because friendship requires action. It doesn't happen passively . . . particularly in today's busy world. Just as we have to make an intentional choice to sit down and spend time with Jesus in order to know Him, we also have to purposefully sit down with friends. In order to truly know others and be known by them, we have to invest time. It won't happen automatically or on the run.

Today's technology allows us to make contact wherever we are, and that can be great. It opens up the world so we can connect with people who are far away. Skyping with your daughter who's on a missions trip to Costa Rica or your son who is serving in Afghanistan or your friend who's working in Hong Kong is an enormous gift. So technology can be a great tool for connection. But it can also isolate us when it becomes a substitute for real relationships.

In our world of "connectivity," many people are sitting alone in front of their computers. They have lots of virtual friends but no real ones. They play games online with anonymous individuals, chatting with avatars in a context where you never quite know if people really are who they say they are.

When Lee and I were newly married, some great friends invited us to become part of a "supper club." Modeled on one friend's parents' experience for many decades, the idea was that seven committed couples would get together for dinner about once a month until we all died.

In the beginning our suppers were epicurean experiences in which we tried very hard to create gourmet cuisine. None of us had children. We had time to ponder hors d'oeuvres recipes and play with table arrangements.

We eventually bought houses, had children, and became very serious. We read lots of James Dobson books. We failed miserably. Our children learned to walk and talk, and then they talked way too much. We went camping and on missions trips and to the beach. We juggled babysitters and kids' sports schedules. We supported each other through job issues and parents' and siblings' deaths. Cancer. The suicide of a loved one. We suffered loss—together—and our dinner conversations went deep, and hard.

But not all the time. We also discussed politics and many other peculiar things, and the headlines, scandals, issues, and eruptions in the world around us. There were some doozies. As the years went by, we no longer went crazy over the gourmet thing. We were happy just to have scraps of whatever and get together, clinging to one another like survivors on a raft on life's choppy seas.

We've been dining together for almost twenty-five years. In fact, the group is coming over tomorrow night, and there will be the usual din of interruptions, wild laughter, and beating on the table. Some of our kids are in college now. They laugh if they happen to be around and hear us dine, since we're so loud. But they love the supper club, because they've seen that this is how friendship is done. You make time for relationships, and you stick with them. They say they'll have their own supper clubs once they're out on their own. So the generations roll on.

Meanwhile, we are much older than we've ever been. It's a shock. When I look around the dinner table each month, what I see are dear friends, as essential and vibrant as ever. But every once in a while I'll look objectively, not through the lens of love, and I'll think, *Oh my gosh, who are all these old people and why am I one of them?*

Lately we've started taking bets on who will die first. Perhaps that is slightly morbid.

Now, are these the people I like best on the entire planet, carefully brought together by research and points of compatibility through Match.com or something? No. Are they my only friends? No. Do I agree with all their political views? Heck, no. Do I agree with every jot and tittle of their theological views? No.

But I bring up this example of our little supper club because the time invested together over the years has made us a band of sisters and brothers, as dysfunctional and nutty as any biological family, but a family still. I look at these people sitting around the dinner table, and I just plain love them. Hopefully I would lay down my life for any of them.

As C. S. Lewis wrote about friendship in *The Four Loves:*

For a Christian, there are, strictly speaking, no chances. A secret Master of the Ceremonies has been at work. Christ, who said to the disciples "Ye have not chosen me, but I have chosen you," can truly say to every group of Christian friends "You have not chosen one another but I have chosen you for one another." The Friendship is not a reward for our discrimination and good taste in finding one another out. It is the instrument by which God reveals to each the beauties of all the others. They are no greater than the beauties of a thousand other men; by Friendship God opens our eyes to them. . . . [As we] feast it is He who has spread the board and it is He who has chosen the guests. It is He, we may dare to hope, who sometimes does, and always should, preside. Let us not reckon without our Host.[1]

Yes. We sit at the table, knit together somehow, friends with each other because we're friends with God—and He is our Host.

Stay
{obey}

21
{Keeping Pace}

Since we live by the Spirit, let us keep in step with the Spirit.

GALATIANS 5:25

So coming to Jesus means we need to learn to sit—with Him, and with friends. We also need to consider another verb of the spiritual life that leads to the promise of rest. This is Jesus' command to "Stay!"

This is not like "STAY," the dog command. Usually when I tell my dog Gus to stay, it has to do with the fact that I am leaving him, as in, I'm exiting the house to go do interesting things and no, he cannot come with me. So I tell him to stay so he won't go bounding out the front door and into the street and be killed by a random, passing Suburban. Then he hangs out at the window for a while, watching me leave, his tail waving sadly good-bye, his furry heart broken. One second later he forgets about me and zones out on the sofa until I return.

Jesus' call for us to stay, which is based in John 15, is a lot more active. Here's an illustration.

For whatever reason, I am not a fan of chick flicks or romantic comedies. I like historical movies with strong protagonists. These usually end up being rather violent, considering that history itself is so. Oh well.

If you saw the movie *Gladiator* years ago, you may remember its opening sequence. The film is set during the time that the mighty Roman Empire stretched from the deserts of Africa to the borders of northern England. More than a quarter of the world's population is subject to the rule of the Caesars . . . and in the winter of AD 180 there is a key battle between Rome and the holdout barbarian tribes in Germany.

As *Gladiator* opens, the chief Roman general, Maximus, a decent, strong leader played wonderfully by Russell Crowe, is contemplating the cold, muddy battlefield. He has set up the battle strategy with his generals. They are prepared to unleash their vast weaponry of war against the less-equipped Germans. The Roman victory is only a matter of time . . . and the loss of many lives, on both sides.

"Strength and honor," Maximus pledges to his generals who will manage the infantry attack. His loyal wolf running by his side, our hero rides on his magnificent horse to join the waiting cavalry in the forest. Once the ground troops attack, Maximus will lead the cavalry to sweep down behind the Germans and decimate their ranks.

Maximus arrives in the forest. Leaning forward in his saddle, swathed in rich fur, his Roman breastplate gleaming, he rallies his men with a final speech before the battle.

"Hold the lines," he shouts to them. "Stay with me! If you find yourself alone riding in green fields with the sun on your face, do not be troubled . . . for you are already dead!"

The hardened warriors laugh.

"Brothers!" Maximus concludes. "What we do in life echoes in eternity!"

The men cheer and beat their shields with their swords.

Meanwhile, at the front of the battle, the imperial archers are unleashing their flaming arrows and death-filled catapults toward the Germans. Under this covering fire, the Roman infantry begins to advance.

Maximus leads his cavalrymen onward as well. They ride in a broad line, almost shoulder to shoulder, then gain speed. Now they are galloping in a horde through the forest toward the rear of the unsuspecting German foot soldiers.

"Stay with me!" Maximus shouts hoarsely to his men as they gallop. "Hold the line! Stay with me! *Stay* with me!"

The cavalry holds the line, bearing down on their enemy from behind and trapping them. The Romans engulf and quickly defeat the Germans.

You may not be a fan of violent historical movies. But keep that picture in your head: the galloping horses, the common cause, the strong leader, the loyal troops, and the command: "STAY WITH ME!"

This is what I mean by the idea of staying with Jesus.

Stay is an active verb . . . not passive. Staying with Jesus is never passive. It is galloping, straining, exulting, and keeping pace with the One who is in charge. It is attentively waiting for the leader's command, which, as any soldier can tell you, is hard. It requires a constant, dogged obedience on our part, what theologian Francis Schaeffer called "passive activity."

"You and I have the possibility every moment of our lives to hand ourselves to the Lord," Schaeffer wrote in his commentary on Romans. "[The command to] 'Yield yourselves' (6:13) is an 'active passivity.' People are naturally afraid of what is only passive, but we should be afraid of what is only active as well. Our calling is to active passivity. God will bring about our sanctification, but we are called to be active partners in the process as we yield ourselves to Him."[1]

Staying with Him in this active yet passive way is organic and mysterious. I was in Jerusalem a while ago and walked among the olive trees in the Garden of Gethsemane. They are 2,000 years old. They were slender saplings in Jesus' day, but olive trees, like people, get fatter as they age. Now they have gnarled, huge trunks that look like props from *The Lord of the Rings* movies. But they are alive. I was told that they still bear olives to this very day—olives that are harvested ceremonially by one ancient family in Jerusalem and are still pressed into rich, fragrant oil.

There are days when we look and feel like "dead" olive trees—days when it seems impossible that any life could flow from our gnarled, calloused lives. But God does miracles. As we stay in Jesus, grafted into Him and flowing with His life rather than our own, we can bear fruit that will last . . . and we will find rest for our souls.

22

{Stay for Love}

As Jesus stepped into the boat,
the man who had been demon-possessed begged him,
"Let me stay with you."

MARK 5:18 GW

Jesus' command for us to "stay" is rooted in John 15. As you know, this passage is part of the powerful, poignant account of Jesus' last words to His disciples just before Judas betrayed Him, just before Jesus was arrested and dragged away to torture and death.

That night at dinner, Jesus' friends could not fully understand what He was saying. But today we have the vantage point of Christ's resurrection, ascension into heaven, and then the arrival of the Holy Spirit, the Helper Jesus talks about repeatedly during His discourse.

Here are a few of the "greatest hits" from these chapters:

I will pray the Father, and He will give you another Helper, that He may abide with you forever. *John 14:16* NKJV

Abide in me, and I in you. As the branch cannot bear fruit by itself, unless it abides in the vine, neither can you, unless you abide in me. *John 15:4* ESV

I am the vine, you are the branches. Whoever abides in me and I in him, he it is that bears much fruit for apart from me you can do nothing. *John 15:5* ESV

If anyone does not abide in me, he is thrown away like a branch and withers; and the branches are gathered, thrown into the fire, and burned. *John 15:6* ESV

If you abide in me, and my words abide in you, ask whatever you wish, and it will be done for you. *John 15:7* ESV

As the Father has loved me, so I have loved you. Abide in my love. *John 15:9* ESV

If you keep my commandments, you will abide in my love, just as I have kept my Father's commandments and abide in his love. *John 15:10* ESV

What do these things mean? What does it really mean to *abide* in Jesus? What does that really look like in your life or mine?

I wish I could say, *Look, here's what we all need to do to understand what Jesus was saying.* There was a time in my spiritual journey when I would have looked for a clear, prescriptive answer, as in a diagram: okay, this is precisely what Jesus meant, and so here's exactly what you and I need to *do*.

But the older I get, the more I embrace the mystery of it all. I love cognitive answers, believe me . . . but a lot of what Jesus told people goes beyond just an intellectual understanding. It's more mysterious . . . but by mystery, I don't mean that it turns into something incoherent or beyond reason. It becomes, if anything, *more* reasonable. More clear, not just to the mind, but the soul. More paradoxical, something that is both counterintuitive and deeply, deeply intuitive.

As we said earlier, the Greek translation of the word that Jesus used here, *meno*, means to stay, to abide, to remain. Used in reference to a place, it means to sojourn or tarry there, not to leave; to dwell. In reference to time, it means to continue to be present, to last, to endure. In reference to a state or condition, it means to remain, not to become another or different.

Many of Jesus' followers left Him during His earthly ministry because His message was too hard, too confusing, too different

from what people had hoped the Messiah—their Deliverer—
would say.

We can leave Him too. We come initially in a rush of delight
to hear this One who calls us, this One who calls our very souls
and loves us with the desperate love we crave.

But what now? Will you stay? Will you *remain*, not just with
Him but *in* Him? Will you actually lose yourself in this relationship that can sweep over you like an ocean? Will you open yourself totally to the Lover of your soul who has fought the forces of
evil and hell to rescue you, His beloved?

I am speaking in these poetic terms because I feel like it's not
my job here to try to deliver yet another exegesis or theological
interpretation of John 15. The Scripture is before us; ample com-
mentaries are available. If we have ears to hear and hearts that
are open, the only question is, are we *willing* to enter into this
mysterious relationship?

Are we willing to remain *in* Him? Grafted, connected all the
time, not just on Sundays or when we feel like it? Are we willing
to give our very selves to someone so powerful and holy that He
is mysterious and frightening as well as good?

I began this book with the assumption that we *will* give ourselves to something, one master or another. I would submit here
that we may as well throw our whole selves into this endeavor
with Jesus . . . and He will show us, each of us, beyond the com-
mentaries and the careful analysis and the word studies—great as
those things are—what it means to *stay* with Him.

What if you said, for thirty days, "Lord, show me what it means
to stay with You, to remain in You, to abide in You? Show me!"

If Abraham was a human person, just like us, and said to God, show me Your glory, and God did, so kindly as to not kill Abraham but give Him as much as he could stand, surely God will meet you and me right where we are if we truly say to Him, "Lord, show us how to stay, dwell, abide, remain, live *in* You!"

I do know one thing. It's so easy for us to settle for less. Maybe to others we look like we're staying with Jesus, but in reality we are cold and distant from Him.

Here's an illustration.

In recent winters Washington, DC, has had some unusual snowstorms. The mother of them all a year or two ago was called "Snowmaggedon." The snow started falling lightly, then steadily. The winds picked up, the temperature dropped, and it kept snowing . . . and snowing . . . and snowing.

Sure, we have snowplows here, and everyone had mobbed stores getting bread and milk and shovels . . . but we were simply not prepared for an event of this magnitude. We're not a hardcore snow town like Buffalo or all those cities in Wisconsin where you have to put a heating pad on your car and talk tenderly to it all night in order for it to start in the morning.

Schools closed. Life came to a stop. The federal government closed for a week. No one noticed. There was snow up to my waist on our deck. Our dog Gus went outside to do his business and we didn't see him again until springtime.

The blizzard knocked out power for millions of us . . . and that's when it started to get interesting. Our teenagers were absolutely flummoxed by this development. No computer or TV or cell phone chargers. As the storm continued, our house got colder and colder. We got out blankets, candles, and flashlights. We melted snow on the gas stove for water.

You know, with the power off, we could still do things. We could get dressed. We could sleep. We could eat . . . not well, but we weren't going to starve to death. We couldn't shower: no hot water. So we were kind of dirty. We were cold. But we could function, sort of, during the day. At night we were pretty helpless. But you could almost get used to creeping around, melting snow on the gas on the stove, cold and gray.

Obviously this is an imperfect metaphor, but here's my point: Without power, we could sort of function. But the reality was, we had NO POWER. It's like our life with Christ. If we aren't plugged in to Him, we have no power.

And once the power came back on in Vaughn World, we were absolutely ecstatic. Hot water: we got clean! We got warm, happy, thankful!

No one who has lived with the power on would ever even consider going back to a little, limited gray life without power.

But that's what we do all the time spiritually.

We settle for so little. "Oh no, this is fine. Sure, I'm cold and stressed and sad and unable to do much, but that's okay. Oh well." "Come near to God," the Scriptures say, "and he will come near to you" (James 4:8).

COME! Let's not be satisfied with a cold, gray world when we could be living in bright, bold, HD color. Plug in to Jesus and stay with Him . . . and you will bear fruit!

Fruit?

What did Jesus mean?

Jesus was talking to people who lived in an agrarian society. They could readily picture ripe, full clusters of grapes on a vine. They knew how the master vinedresser would come along, pruning healthy, productive branches so they would bear even more fruit. They could see the husbandman cutting off the branches that may have looked nice but were barren.

It's a little harder for us to visualize all this. If you're like me, you get your grapes at the grocery store, encased in a little plastic bag with holes in it.

Basically, Jesus was saying there are two kinds of branches.

The first is those who believe in Him, yes, but that's as far as it goes. They may be church members; they may seem to do all the right things, singing praise songs with great gusto and showing up at meetings.

It's interesting that Jesus talked about this right after Judas Iscariot had gone out into the night to gather the people who had bribed him to betray Jesus. He would return in just a while to hand Jesus over to the people who would have Him killed. But up to that point Judas had *looked* like a disciple. He was a branch in Jesus' vine, so to speak.

But he was not interested in the glory of God. He was, at heart, interested in the advancement of Judas. He was a dead branch. And, as Jesus said, he was cast out . . . and thrown into the fire.

"A good tree cannot bear bad fruit, and a bad tree cannot bear good fruit," Jesus had said a year or two earlier. "Every tree that does not bear good fruit is cut down and thrown into the fire. Thus, by their fruit you will recognize them" (Matthew 7:18–20).

Pretty sobering.

The people who bear fruit are the ones who are truly desiring the glory of God, not self. They are the ones who "abide" in Jesus, coming to Him, sitting with Him, staying with Him, absorbing His Word, connecting with Him in prayer, becoming, in fact, like Him.

When we become like Him, all of our energies, desires, talents, time, and treasure become strangely devoted to the glory of God. Life becomes a wild feast of extravagance . . . not gorging ourselves, no, but wildly and joyously expending everything we have for God's pleasure. The poorest person you know can do this. So can the richest. So can we.

For these rollicking people who are full of a crazy love for God, a severe mercy exists.

Jesus said that God in fact prunes each branch that is bearing fruit. Why? Getting pruned is pretty painful for the prune-ee. But branches won't bear more fruit unless they're pruned. If you've ever trimmed back leggy plants in your garden, you know just how this works. The plant wants to go longer and farther from the source of its energy; but if you prune it, it becomes bushy and jovial and full of fruit.

These people are under the influence of Jesus. We're used to thinking about people driving under the influence of alcohol and other substances; they do what the drug leads them to do. If we're under the influence of Jesus, we'll do what He leads us to do. We will "keep His commandments," as He put it in John 15. We will enter into the cycle of love, or the dance of grace . . . receiving love and grace from the Son who makes us acceptable to the Father, living by the power of the Holy Spirit, inspired and empowered to do what Jesus would do.

When we're in that state, we will bear fruit. It just happens.

What is the fruit? Well, if you are growing out of a grapevine, you'll bear grapes. If you are growing out of the Jesus-vine, you will bear His fruit: love. We receive the sap of love, so to speak, and that in turn goes out to what we make for others so they can be accepted, nourished, refreshed.

Jesus said that it is "fruit that will last." This is eternal. Us yielding fruit through the power of Jesus will in turn draw people to know Him. That way they will live eternally.

This leads to the ultimate goal—the chief end of human beings—which is to glorify God and enjoy Him forever. Everything we do is to be to the glory of God . . . and as we begin to experience that as our norm, under the influence of the Spirit, who has the same goal, we will begin to live in a truly fruitful way.

The world, the flesh, and the devil will always tempt us to pursue things for our own glory . . . so people will think we are clever, or funny, or smart, or spiritually mature. This is a trap, a tiresome cul-de-sac of anxiety. We are freed from it when we truly get that, oh my gosh, everything I am and have is all for the one purpose of bringing glory to God! How do I stay with Him? It's not about duty, but love! How can I do that today, in the next five minutes, in traffic, with this difficult colleague or this child or this neighbor, or this whatever?

This way of thinking and living turns life into a fresh adventure, not a careful protection of the big, stale Self who lurks in all of us, sitting there on a stupid throne like Jabba the Hutt, waving fat short arms and demanding attention.

What is your life about? What is my life about? We can noodle that forever, or we can say, like Paul, *Oh God, all I know is that by the grace of God, I am what I am, and Your grace to me did not prove vain* (see 1 Corinthians 15:10). *Trim away the things that suck me dry, and let me thrive in You.*

There's a lot more we could say; this is a huge topic. On the other hand, it's pretty simple. Pray something like that and see what happens. It will be radical, which literally means, after all, to return to the root: Jesus.

23

{Unleashed!}

*Sin shall no longer be your master,
because you are not under law, but under grace.
You have been set free from sin and
have become slaves to righteousness.*

ROMANS 6:14, 18

*I shall run the way of Your commandments,
for You will enlarge my heart.*

PSALM 119:32 NASB

Last April, I was at a friend's cottage at the ocean. It was before the official start of the tourist season . . . which meant that our dog could run free on the beach, off-leash.

Gus is a suburban dog; beyond the fenced dog park and the fenced backyard, he's not used to running free. He couldn't believe his good fortune.

I walked down to the beach, released him from the leash, and he was astonished. He ran in wild circles like a demented sheepdog, churning the sand and barking at the waves. Seagulls scattered. Sandpipers skittered. Crabs watched him go by, waving their small claws and holding their big claws in reserve.

Once Gus had settled down a bit and could walk in straight lines, we proceeded down the beach, parallel to the water. It was glorious. Freedom for the dog and for me as well. Big waves, blue sky, no other people. We walked for miles.

If you're not a dog person, this won't make much sense to you perhaps, but if you are a dog person, you get it. There is such a sense of mutual pleasure when you're walking along with your dog, not having to restrain him on a leash.

The dog is happy: he is free. He could run away, of course, but he chooses to stay close. He trusts you. If mean dogs or sharks come, you are there for him.

And you are happy: he is fulfilling the essence of his dog-ness, running with great joy in the wind, next to the waves. He will come if you call. He knows there are boundaries. You, as master, feel the pleasure of his freedom and his obedience, his connection and compliance and trust in you. He loves you. That's why he stays with you.

I would shyly submit that this is the same kind of dynamic in our relationship with God. He designed us to be free . . . this is why we weren't pre-programmed in the Garden of Eden to only do the Right Thing. If that had been the case, we would have been scary automatons or robots. But we are human beings with a choice to be in love with God and come to Him as Master—or not. We can submit in obedience to Him and stay close, without the leash of the Law.

We seem to have an intrinsic, built-in need to belong to someone.

I thought of this when I was on a black-sand beach in Costa Rica a few months ago. We were near a poor village, and there were about five or six mangy dogs that followed us on the beach. They were strays with matted coats, covered with dirt. One of them was missing an eye. They didn't belong to anyone. They were free. But they were not happy dogs. They begged us, in dog-Spanish, to take them home. They needed the care of a good master.

To further understand the kind of care that Jesus offers, consider Matthew 11:28–30 again: "Come to me, all you who are weary and burdened, and I will give you rest. Take my yoke upon you and learn from me, for I am gentle and humble in heart, and you will find rest for your souls. For my yoke is easy and my burden is light."

We've already talked about the weights and burdens that the Pharisees piled on people. Jesus was as different from these religious leaders as He could be. He was saying, "Come to Me . . . it's not about rules, it's about a *relationship!*"

If I may, He was saying, "Come to Me, and I will give you rest. I will help you, come alongside you, take on with you the burdens that you must bear, and take OFF the ones you don't need to carry. You don't have to do 613 things to be holy and acceptable to Me. Just one thing: *Come.* Take My yoke."

What the heck is a yoke? What did He mean by that, really? Is it the heavy burden of shoulds I described in an earlier chapter? Is it that if we take on all the right behaviors and perform just as He wants, *then* He'll give us rest and relief?

That makes no sense.

Probably like most people in North American suburbia, I've never seen a yoke in actual use except in Colonial Williamsburg, and that doesn't count. So the following story helps me visualize what's going on with the yoke.

A pastor was watching an old farmer plowing a field with a team of oxen. One was a huge ox and the other a small bullock. The ox towered over the little bullock that was sharing the work with him.

The pastor didn't understand the inequality until he was told, "See the way the traces are hooked into the yoke? You will observe that the large ox is pulling all the weight. That little bullock is being broken in to the yoke, but he is not actually pulling any weight."

The pastor, of course, thought about Matthew 11:28–30, reflecting, "In the normal yoking, the load is equally distributed between the two that are yoked together, but when we are yoked with Jesus Christ, He bears the load, and we who are yoked to

Him share in the joy and the accomplishment of the labor but without the burden of the yoke."[1]

It's a beautiful yet counterintuitive picture. Yokes have a negative connotation: they are heavy and often refer to loads of oppression, slavery, or legalism. But Jesus was telling the people of His day—and us—that *His* yoke is unique. Yes, there is responsibility; there are boundaries. Yes, there are fields to be plowed with the seed of His gospel. But it is a yoke lined with love, as Bible commentator Matthew Henry put it. Jesus binds Himself in with us, pulls our loads, and shows us how to grow stronger in Him as we learn of Him by watching Him, working with Him, walking with Him, and staying with Him.

There is a big difference between a yoke and a leash. Jesus doesn't have us on a chain, jerking us around. His image of this wedded relationship is that we are joined with Him, pulling together.

Conversely, the Law—as the Pharisees had used it to manipulate the Jewish people—was a huge leash, yanking them into line. But God's plan was one of freedom . . . not law, leashes, cattle prods, or anything like that. No mastery by intimidation or force. No tedious checklists of rules and regulations. No constant questioning about "Am I good enough? Have I been careful enough? Have I done enough?" No anxiety about life's end, wondering if the cosmic scales will show that I have done more good than bad.

No, God made a plan where people could become His willing servants. We connect with our Master off-leash, if you will, free and in trusting connection with Him. We can run the way of His commandments, for He will actually enlarge our hearts, as Psalm 119:32 puts it. We can have the real freedom that comes from obedience. We can know the true security that He is always with us and that whatever threats we may encounter along the way—discouragement, death, or Satan himself—our Master is stronger.

24
{Jesus, Stay with Us!}

Who is the third who walks always beside you?

—T. S. ELIOT, *"The Waste Land"*

These last few chapters have focused on the idea of us staying with Jesus. There's a corollary that's worth noting: once we have met Him, we want *Him* to stay with us.

I love the story from Luke 24 that illustrates this. It takes place after Jesus' crucifixion, and after His resurrection too, but the disciples don't yet understand that Jesus has risen from the dead.

The action picks up on a dirt road. Two of Jesus' bedraggled disciples are trudging along. One is Cleopas, and some commentators believe his companion was his wife, whom we will call Mrs. Cleopas. They are heading from Jerusalem to a village called Emmaus. It's about a seven-mile walk. The couple is absolutely shattered. Their leader has been crucified; their friends are in hiding. All is lost, and their voices break as they talk about the horrors of the past few days.

Then a man joins them on the road. He's swathed in a robe. He falls into step with them. They don't recognize that it's Jesus.

"What are these things you're discussing?" He asks.

They stop and stare at Him. How could anybody in that area not know about Jesus' arrest and crucifixion? Jerusalem has been in an uproar for days, with earthquakes, darkness, and chaos in the streets. Where has this yokel been?

"Are You the only person around here who isn't aware of all the things that have been going on?" Cleopas asks. He is peeved.

Then comes the most exquisitely ironic verse in all Scripture.

Jesus Christ looks at Cleopas, His eyebrows up, His voice casual, and says: "What things?"

This is *Jesus* talking.

What things?

Are you kidding me?

You can imagine the reaction of the angels who are watching, peeking out from the party realms of heaven.

They're filled with wonder and joy. They know that Satan has been dealt the death blow. You know how you can laugh so easily when you're happy? So I imagine that when Jesus, with perfect timing, asks the clueless Cleopas couple, *"What things?"* that all of heaven explodes in a wild tumult: huge peals of perfect, joyful laughter.

The great British author G. K. Chesterton wrote, "We sit perhaps in a starry chamber of silence, while the laughter of the heavens is too loud for us to hear. Joy, which was the small publicity of the pagan, is the gigantic secret of the Christian."

Chesterton continues, saying that Jesus restrained or concealed one aspect of His personality during His time on earth. It wasn't His tears or His anger.

> He never concealed his tears; He showed them plainly on His open face at any daily sight. . . . He never restrained His anger. He flung furniture down the front steps of the Temple, and asked men how they expected to escape the damnation of Hell.
>
> Yet He restrained something. . . . I say it with reverence: there was in that shattering personality a thread that must be called shyness. . . . There was something that He covered constantly by abrupt silence or impetuous isolation.

There was some one thing that was too great for God to show us when He walked upon our earth; and I have sometimes fancied that it was His mirth.[1]

Ah, yes, the laughter of the heavens, and of Jesus Christ Himself! One day we will hear it, and we will laugh out loud right with Him!

But Mr. and Mrs. Cleopas couldn't yet hear it. They just stood there on the dusty road when Jesus asked them His funny question. They were so sad. They told Jesus the whole story about Jesus of Nazareth and how they had put their hopes in Him, but He had been crucified. To complicate things even further, they told Jesus, now some of the women in their group were saying that Jesus had actually risen from the dead . . . but when the menfolk had checked things out, they hadn't seen Him.

Whoa, says Jesus, though of course they don't yet know it's Him. He takes them through the ultimate Bible study, explaining all the prophecies concerning Himself, showing them how Messiah had to suffer before He could enter into His glory.

For the first time, these disciples of Jesus are really seeing the truth of how Jesus fulfilled Scripture.

They arrive at their village. Jesus "acted as if He were going farther," the Bible says.

Who knew Jesus was such a great actor?

Cleopas and Mrs. C. beg Him, saying "Stay with us!"

The word "stay" is also translated as "abide." "Abide with us!" they asked Jesus . . . just as He had told the disciples, four nights earlier at the Last Supper, "Abide in Me!"

So He did. You know the rest of the story: Jesus broke bread at the table with them, and when He blessed it, their eyes were opened and they recognized it was Him. Then He vanished, something His resurrected body was able to do.

Mr. and Mrs. C. say to each other, Oh my goodness, honey, "did not our hearts *burn* within us while he talked to us on the road, while he opened to us the Scriptures?" (Luke 24:32 ESV). And then, even though it's dark outside and no one back then traveled at night, they jumped up and run all the way back to Jerusalem, their blazing hearts pumping like pistons the whole way.

You and I wish we could have that literal experience. *Jesus, stay with us!* We wish we could actually hear Him explaining His Word to us.

One day we will.

But for now, we need to somehow see with eyes of faith. This One who said, "I will never leave you or forsake you," in fact walks with us on every dusty road of our life journey. God with us. *Immanuel.* He has stayed with us, He is staying with us, He will stay with us. Forever.

Rest

{trust and blessing}

25

{The Rest of the Story}

Thou hast made us for Thyself, O Lord,
and our heart is restless
until it finds its rest in Thee.

ST. AUGUSTINE, *Confessions*

So long as we are occupied with any other object than God Himself,
there will be neither rest for the heart nor peace for the mind. But
when we receive all that enters our lives as from His hand, then, no
matter what may be our circumstances or surroundings—whether
in a hovel or prison-dungeon, or at a martyr's stake—we shall be
enabled to say, "The lines are fallen unto me in pleasant places" (Ps.
16:6). But that is the language of faith, not of sight nor of sense.

A. W. PINK, *The Sovereignty of God*

If you're like me, maybe you haven't really focused on the "rest" that Jesus is talking about in Matthew 11. I've always thought of it as, well, you know, *rest*. Repose. I just skim right over it, because it sounds wonderful and I think I know what that means. Peace. Quietness of spirit. Refreshment of soul and mind. Physical invigoration.

And of course, all that is true. Bring it on!

But there is a deeper and even more significant meaning to Jesus' words. If we understand it well, it can actually revolutionize our daily experience. I believe it is one of the great secrets of faith and a major missing piece in many believers' lives today.

In his writing on this passage, Pastor Ray Stedman said there are two promises of rest in Jesus' invitation of Matthew 11:28–30.

The first, as we said in chapter 6, is the relief of salvation, the rest that comes from being delivered of the damning burden of sin and guilt that will otherwise cast us into an eternity of restless shame.

This rest is *given*, free of charge, without our needing to earn it or somehow "be worthy" of it. Those who rest on Jesus' saving work on the cross know that He did the work to achieve it. We could not.

This kind of rest is pretty exhilarating.

But exhilaration fades, because our human nature has an unfortunate default. We tend to drift away from God and forget His great mercies. If we're not walking with Him, we're walking away from Him. There's no such thing as spiritual "neutral."

We are also affected by our emotions. We're subject to what C. S. Lewis called the "law of undulation." Regardless of how even our keels might be, we all have highs and lows, bright days and dark nights of the soul. Sometimes we simply plod through gray periods when the fire in our hearts has faded and our emotions have ebbed. We feel tired and disillusioned so we try harder, beating our brains out with more activity, longer to-do lists, and all kinds of good stuff. We end up feeling even more dull and unsatisfied.

In terms of our eternal destiny, yes, we're already resting in Jesus for our salvation. That's taken care of. But we need an ongoing sense of His rest that gives holy refreshment and peace to our everyday lives.

This second rest is in the latter part of Jesus' words in Matthew 11: "Take my yoke upon you, and learn from me . . . and *you will find rest.*"

If the first rest is *given* by God, this second rest is *found* by the believer.[1]

To really understand the incredible nature of this rest, and to be able to find it so we can experience it, we need to understand the biblical meaning of *shabbat.*

The Hebrew word *shabbat* means to "rest or stop or cease from work." God instituted this when, according to the creation account in Genesis 2, He "rested on the seventh day from all His work" of making everything from hummingbirds to walruses to galaxies, gravity, grapes, and human beings.

Was God tired, and that's why He needed to rest?

No. If God is who the Scriptures proclaim Him to be, He is almighty and all-powerful. He is "the everlasting God, the Creator of the ends of the earth. He will not grow tired or weary," as Isaiah 40:28 puts it.

It's interesting: "seven," "Sabbath," and "rest" are all the same basic word in Hebrew—*shabbat*. This is also very close to the meaning of the Hebrew *shalom*: deep peace, right relationships with God, and right relationships with others. The *shabbat* of Genesis means that God ceased from work. On the seventh day, He stopped what He was doing.

Why?

He was finished with His work.

When God made man and woman, the original work of Creation was done. Once reasoning, thinking, in-God's-image man was created, it does not appear that we humans have evolved into anything further, except some teenagers who seem to have turned into slugs, but that's another story.

God finished His work of Creation. He rested. And He gave His shiny new people His gift of rest. They had no worries or anxieties of any kind. Their needs were met, they lived in a garden paradise, and they had perfect connection with God and each other. No regrets about the past nor any fears about the future. They lived in the present: the gift of God's rest.

But sadly, as we saw earlier, Adam and Eve believed Satan's lies rather than reveling in God's truth. And when they sinned, they lost their rest. They entered into a sad state of restlessness, shame, sin, and pain. They knew what it was to hide and deceive; they became intimately acquainted with regret and fear.

But God did not abandon them. He provided a way for human beings to re-enter His rest through the eventual work of

His Son. And in His covenant relationship with Israel, when God instituted the practice of a weekly Sabbath—a day of rest—for the Jewish people, it was just a picture of the ultimate rest that would come when the Messiah's work of *redemption* was done. The Old Testament practice of sacrifices was a picture of the ultimate sacrifice when Jesus would come and pay the sin-debt of human beings with His own blood, poured out as redemption for many.

As Ray Stedman put it, "These Old Testament shadows were looking forward to the coming of the One who would fulfill these and thus end them. When the work of Jesus Christ was finished, the shadows were no longer needed."[2] So when Jesus hung on the cross and declared, just before He died, "It is finished," and then rose again, the Sabbath was no longer needed. The picture of resting from the work, once a week, was done because the work of atonement was finished. So followers of Jesus started worshiping God on the day of resurrection, when Jesus had come out of the tomb.

Further, all the works prescribed by the Law were no longer needed. No more sacrifices: Jesus was the ultimate Atonement. No need to keep kosher or meticulously try so hard to follow the rules of the Pharisees. All those works were now unnecessary. Human beings could "rest" from all our concentrated efforts to make ourselves acceptable to God.

As Tim Keller says:

At the end of his great act of creation, the Lord said, "It is finished," and he could rest. On the cross at the end of his great act of redemption Jesus said, "It is finished"—and we can rest. On the cross Jesus was saying of the work underneath your work—the thing that makes you truly weary, this need to prove yourself because who you are and what you do are never good enough—that is finished. He has lived the life you should have lived, he has died the death you should have died. If you rely on Jesus's finished work, you know that God is satisfied with you. You can be satisfied with life.[3]

As Hebrews 4:9–10 puts it, "There remains, then, a Sabbath-rest for the people of God; for anyone who enters God's rest also rests from their works, just as God did from his."

This rest is ours, of course, as "the gift of God—not by works, so that no one can boast" (Ephesians 2:8).

Do you see what this means?

It's not just some dusty theological thought about the Sabbath that only ancient Jews would understand. It means that when we believe in Jesus' finished work on the cross, we can *rest* from all our striving efforts. Like God "resting" after creation, we rest from our works, because the work is done. We stop. We cease. We don't need to do anything.

This is why the apostle Paul said, "I no longer live, but Christ lives in me" (Galatians 2:20). This is why Jesus said in John 14, "The Son can do nothing by himself" (John 5:19). This is why believers know that "it is God who works in you, both to will and to work for his good pleasure" (Philippians 2:13 esv).

Ray Stedman said, "The secret of true Christian life is to cease from dependence on one's own activity, and to *rest in dependence upon the activity of Another* who dwells within. That is fulfilling the Sabbath, the true Sabbath."[4] This can set us free. Just as our salvation is done, finished by Christ at the cross, so is our striving and trying and working and pushing and agonizing over what we haven't done. It's all done! We can rest in Jesus' work, because it is complete.

So, we all say, does this mean I don't have to do anything? Am I just a blob? Do I lie around eating pistachios and waiting for God to do great things?

We may well be blobs, but we're *God's* blobs, and He has plenty of fun work for us to do.

The radical secret here is a change in our *motivation*, or *why we do things*. We don't toil to achieve God's favor. We don't do good things so other people will like us. We aren't driven to labor with excellence in our jobs, homes, churches, and communities because our self-image comes from our achievements.

No. We are resting in Christ's finished work on the cross. He suffered cosmic restlessness in our place. Now our motivation for doing anything is gratitude and exuberant love. Now we can work with eager abandon and great expectations, because we don't have to worry about how things will turn out. It's all for His glory—not ours—and we know that the outcomes of our ministry, labor, and efforts are all in *God's* hands . . . and we trust Him.

When we live in this secret, we are free. We're no longer driven by that insane need to do well in our work so that we'll feel good about ourselves. Our emotions no longer fluctuate with our approval ratings. We're no longer restless, crazily controlled by that need to check off every item on our very long to-do list.

Interestingly, it is this rest that allows us to bear fruit. As branches rooted in the Jesus vine, we're not trying, trying, pushing, pushing, sweating in our grape labor to bear big clusters of fruit.

Again, if we understand the Sabbath blessing of rest, the work is done. When that was the case in the Garden of Eden, after Creation was complete, God told the animals to "be fruitful and multiply." And before the Fall, God told Adam and Eve to "be fruitful and multiply, and have dominion over the earth." The result of rest is fruit.

Apart from resting in Jesus, we can do nothing. All our works, all our effort, will yield nothing of lasting value. Resting in His completed work, we *will* bear His fruit: Love for people we don't even like. Joy in tough times, peace in chaos. Patience in frustrating circumstances. Kindness to those who dismay us. Goodness. Faithfulness. Gentleness. Self-control. This is supernatural. Such things are the fruit of the Spirit of God (Galatians 5:22), wrought by the Son of God through the authority of God the Father.

This journey of being a Christ-follower isn't about trying harder and being more disciplined. I once heard a Christian consultant talk about how we are to be like pencils, sharpened and ready to do God's work.

In a certain sense that's true . . . but to me it sounded too much like the world around us. We live in a society in which value, status, and identity come from achievement. *What do you do? What's your title? What school did you go to? How much do you make? How sharp are you?*

But the kingdom of God is full of people who know, *Hey, I'm dull! I'm not accomplished! I'm just another bozo on the bus . . . or, as the apostle Paul put it, I'm a fool—for Christ* (see 1 Corinthians 4:10).

Through *any* surrendered life—any humbled person who takes on the yoke of His authority—Jesus Christ can bear great fruit. He has done the work, and His Spirit will cause that work on the cross to take effect all over the world, yielding results wherever He pleases. It is not up to us.

"For we are God's handiwork, created in Christ Jesus to do good works, which God prepared in advance for us to do" (Ephesians 2:10).

Do you see the difference between resting in Jesus' work versus working hard doing our own works?

If we are constantly busy doing things to make ourselves feel good about ourselves, that focus on self will drive us nuts and shrivel our souls. We can do selfless acts—caring for others, volunteering for church committees, helping the poor—for selfish reasons, as in, down deep, I am actually sacrificing here so I will feel good about *me*.

As Tim Keller put it in a wonderful sermon on Hebrews 4, quoting from theologian Richard Lovelace, "The thing that separates believers from a full experience of God and rest in Him is not so much our sins."[5] (Yes, yes, we should repent of our sins. Sin is bad. Don't do it.) But Lovelace says that the things that distance us from God are often our "damnable good works."

The Pharisees did good things. But their hearts were far from God. They got their kicks from what other people thought about them, their social standing, and how well they were playing the tricky game of legalism.

When we're trying to live the Christian life in our own strength, for our own self-validation, we will always be weary, even when we're resting.

When we are living in Jesus—having come to Him, sitting with Him, staying with Him and in Him—then we are always resting, even when we're working.

26

{Free at Last}

It is for freedom that Christ has set us free.
Stand firm, then, and do not let yourselves be burdened
again by a yoke of slavery.

GALATIANS 5:1

You will find rest for your souls," Jesus said.

How?

We find it by taking His yoke.

We talked earlier about Christ's imagery in Matthew 11: the big wooden yoke frequently worn by oxen, but not so often by humans.

So how do we take His figurative yoke?

The yoke is the humility to accept His authority and let Him give the commands in our lives. It is, essentially, dying to the notion of self as master. Once we do this, then we can bear fruit, for as Jesus said, "Unless a grain of wheat falls into the earth and dies, it remains alone; but if it dies, it bears much fruit. Whoever loves his life loses it, and whoever hates his life in this world will keep it for eternal life" (John 12:23–24 ESV).

What are the obstacles?

The main obstacle is huge, and plain. It is pride. It is the self-focus, self-sufficiency, and self-reliance that says, *No, I will not come. I will not bow my head to take anyone else's yoke.*

Let's return to the world of dogs for a moment—to the concept known as the Alpha dog.

In wolf packs, dog groups, and other pack behaviors, the "alpha" is the leader. He often asserts his dominance by aggression; other pack members yield and acknowledge that they are subordinate.

I would submit, as I have earlier in different ways, that God could easily play the heavy here. He could easily blow us to kingdom come, literally. He could overpower us in such a way that there would be no choice but to yield.

But when God Himself came to earth, He did it differently. Jesus didn't intimidate His hearers through a show of dominance, aggression, or by fully revealing His power. Particularly in this passage we've been considering in Matthew, He says something totally surprising. He says, "Take My yoke, because I'm gentle and *meek*."

What?

Gentleness and meekness are not much prized in our society today. The strong survive. Acceptable socialized aggression has been elevated to an art form in business and group interaction, in television "entertainment," as well as in professional and not-so-professional sports. Lots of people still perceive Jesus as that figure many of us grew up with: the pale, wimpy guy with His thin hair parted in the middle. He was always swathed in some girly-looking robe and looked like a good wind would knock Him right over.

Of course, the reality is that Jesus was a swarthy, first-century Jew, a muscular carpenter by trade. Rough fishermen—the manly men of the day—were drawn to Him. People thronged around Him. He slept outside, passed rigorous days, and endured torture in the end. It just does not seem likely that He was some sort of timid fellow who did not want to get His hands dirty.

So what does it mean here when He says He is gentle and meek? For some of us, that feels like a deal-killer. Who wants a commander-in-chief who's gentle and meek and geeky? I don't mean to be crass, but most of us want a kick-butt Savior.

Meekness is one of the least-understood words in our vocabulary. People tend to think of it as weakness, indecision, or lack of confidence. The original Greek word, however, really does not mean "doormat." It means "gentle strength."

Remember, the context in Matthew 28 is that Jesus just said that He had been given all things, or all authority. Though the people to whom He spoke at the time didn't have the full context, we do. This is the absolute Ruler of the universe here, by whose authority the earth itself was created and remains in its orbit in space. This is the One who conquered death and hell. This is the One who braved all horrors to snatch us away from soul death. This is the One who is coming again in some absolute cosmic cataclysmic event in which every eye will see Him and every knee will bow down.

Meekness is not weakness. It is power under control.

So in taking Jesus' yoke, what are we doing? We're admitting our need and recognizing His authority.

Yes, if we want to continue the dog analogy, we're rolling on our backs, vulnerable underbellies exposed, submitting to the Alpha who is also the Omega, first and last. (I would suggest actually adopting that position in times of stillness and prayer—not because I'm weird, but because that physical posture of prayerful submission can actually help humble our souls.) And the great paradox is that as we become meek in this way, submissive to God's will, we become strong. He empowers us through the Holy Spirit.

So let's be clear. Coming to Jesus and taking His yoke is not passivity, the giving up of personality to become a colorless clone. It is the surrender of self-authority, acknowledging Him as the Master. It is an act of humility on our part, but not humiliation.

It is being like Christ, who said to His Father, "Not My will, but Yours be done."

When we do that, we become more ourselves than ever before. As C. S. Lewis said, we don't find ourselves, so to speak, until we are looking only for Christ.

> Until you have given up yourself to Him you will not have a real self. . . . It will come when you are looking for Him. . . . Look for yourself, and you will find in the long run only hatred, loneliness, despair, rage, ruin, and decay. But look for Christ, and you will find Him, and with Him everything else thrown in.[1]

When we submit, play dead, surrender, we will finally find what we've been looking for. It's odd: focusing on Jesus makes us able to truly see who we are. We see that so many of the burdens we've carried are, one way or another, manifestations of self. Preoccupation with self, self-advancement, self-love, selfishness . . . ah, how liberating to be rid of these things! We'll agree with Charles Spurgeon, who put it, "I have now concentrated all my prayers into one, and that one prayer is this, that I may die to self, and live wholly to Him."[2]

And when life is done and time is up, we will never, ever regret letting go of our yipping, tiresome, relentless selves. We will never regret coming to rest in Jesus. We will sing to God Almighty, *Ah, thank You, thank You! Free at last!*

27

{Fun Rest}

Commit your soul to Him, and then fear nothing.

JOHN NEWTON,
The Works of the Rev. John Newton

Religion, works, performance, and having to be so careful and guarded about one's true self: all this is exhausting. But learning to live in the freedom of God's rest is a great adventure.

The religious life is predictable. Yet when we live in intimacy with Jesus, there are surprises around every corner. There is a rollicking sort of uncertainty that is scary . . . but it's fun because we trust that God Himself is in control.

It's sort of like riding a roller coaster that terrifies you, but you trust its design will hold. So you strap yourself in, scream wildly, laugh, and run back to do it again. Absolutely exhilarating. Meanwhile the people who sit out the adventure, safe on the ground, are missing the fun.

If you're not a roller-coaster person, that's fine. It's just an illustration.

The point is that many of us try to play it safe in our spiritual lives. We want to be sure we'll be okay. We fear that if we totally yield to God and trust Him, He'll immediately send us off to become a missionary to Africa. Yet we want to maintain some control.

Oswald Chambers said that we tend to be "so mathematical and calculating that we look upon uncertainty as a bad thing." Certainty, he said, "is the mark of the common-sense life: gracious uncertainty is the mark of the spiritual life. To be certain of God means that we are uncertain in all our ways; we do not know what a day may bring forth. This is generally said with a sigh of sadness; it should be rather an expression of breathless expectation. We are uncertain of the next step, but we are certain of God."[1]

So what do we do?

Sometimes we can cast about thinking, *Oh, my goodness, there are so many needs all around us, all over the world. Gosh, what do we do, where do we go? It's overwhelming. I need to make a plan and wait and pray until I'm certain of God's exact will for me.*

Of course it is good to pray and wait for God's nudge and plan (in that order), but many believers grow stagnant waiting around, trying to figure out God's will for their lives. I've found it's a great principle to start right where God has you, look around, and recognize the opportunities He's already given.

For example, perhaps you've noticed many references to the Dominican Republic in this book. Is this because I've focused on the DR as the place whose people most touch my heart? No. Is it because I've studied poverty charts or human needs or because I'm fluent in Spanish? No, no, and *no, pero me gustaría.*

It's because God has used godly people at our church to spearhead a great movement of His work in the DR, and I believe I have a small part to play in terms of specific ministry there among women in a community of great need. I love these women. I can't wait to see them again and bond with them in Jesus.

So it's not like I decided the Dominican Republic was my very favorite place on the planet. If you gave me a globe and asked, "Gee, where do you care about most in the whole wide world?" I wouldn't point to the DR. But *this* is what God has provided just now, and I try to do what Oswald Chambers suggested: "Abandon to God, and do the duty that lies nearest; He packs our life with surprises all the time."[2]

Our human tendency, as I've said repeatedly, is that we want formulas and an outline to follow. Just show me what we're supposed to do, and I'll do it.

But life in the Spirit is no formula. No rules. Just right. It is a relationship with a living Lord who will live in us and guide us if we yield our precious control to Him.

I was recently in another country with a missionary friend. She is young enough to be my daughter, and yet much more mature and wonderful than me. She was talking about the tension between working and rest. There are so many needs, she said. She could constantly be doing all kinds of great work . . . particularly since one of the ministry outreaches that is bearing great fruit is sharing the gospel with prostitutes so they can come off the street and into a relationship with Jesus. That kind of ministry isn't done on a nine-to-five basis . . . it has more to do with hanging out on the streets and sharing with women at midnight.

My friend has a pastor-husband, also committed to ministry, and small children. How much time does she devote to all the needs around her? One hundred percent to *everything?*

To add to the conundrum, other members of the mission community face the same challenges. Sometimes there are challenges and tension: *Hey, why aren't you guys doing as much ministry as we are?*

The question, my missionary friend said, is when do we beat our brains out for Jesus, like the missionary heroes of olden days? When do we pull back? I need some margin in my life. I need to be with my husband, play with my kids, and occasionally go to bed early. How do I figure out when to do that, and when to be up all night, doing God's work?

This question is more dramatic on the mission field, but it also confronts all of us at home. We live in urgent times. The needs around us are compelling. How do we, as individuals and as the corporate body of Christ, figure out how to respond? What do we need to do? What can we wait on Christ to do?

Sometimes busy people talk about "balance" in their lives. I can't quite figure that out. What are we balancing? Our family or personal health on one side of the scale, work on the other? I don't think it works that way. To me, it's a question of *priorities* and our real connection with the Spirit of God: "Show me what You would have me do just now." In my experience, my priority of 10 a.m. may well be different from my priority of 6 p.m. God can lead us during our days, as in, when to run, when to stop, when to be with family, and when to stride out into fields of service.

Why, oh why isn't there a nice, clear answer to this?

Because if there was a nice formula, then we'd fall into that trap we love: the trap of legalism and measuring how well we're doing, and how well other people are adhering to the clear standard of achievement.

Our clear standard is to love and obey Jesus.

If we're plugged into Him, no matter how messed up we are, we'll hear His Spirit stirring our hearts. As we meditate on it, His Word will jump around on the pages, like it's alive. Which it is. We will somehow *know*, for each one of us, when to go, when to stay, when to sleep, and when to push onward in ministry—as Jesus did.

Charles Spurgeon said that sometimes God makes His servants like birds who rest on the wing: "Taking a mighty flap, they seem to pass mile after mile at every stroke of their wings, resting while flying. Thus you may stretch your pinions of progress, and of holy aspiration, and rise higher and higher, and yet still be at rest!"[3]

I like to think of this kind of "resting" while moving at great speed in a different way.

On October 14, 1947, a military pilot named Chuck Yeager wedged himself into the cockpit of an experimental rocket plane called the XS-1, sitting in the belly of a big B-29 mother ship. Yeager's mission in this top-secret test was to break the sound barrier. British planes that had gotten close to the speed of sound (about 660 miles per hour at 40,000 feet) had shaken violently, bolts rattling and controls buffeting. Pilots had always throttled down at that point; one who did not had been blown to bits. No one knew for sure whether a plane could fly faster than the speed of sound, also known as Mach 1.

The B-29 climbed to 20,000 feet, and then pilot Yeager's plane was dropped out of the bomb bay. Its four rockets firing, the small airplane started shaking violently. Jolting, swaying, heaving, Yeager hung in there, still pushing the throttle forward. The Mach needle edged up past 0.965, and then it went off the scale.

The men on the ground heard a huge, thunderous bang. Was it Yeager's plane exploding, as had happened to another test pilot? No. It was the very first sonic boom, the roar of a plane surpassing the speed of sound.

Yeager was flying supersonic, something no human being had yet done. The plane's shaking and heaving stopped. "It was as smooth as a baby's bottom," he said later. "Grandma could be sitting up there sipping lemonade." Ease. Quiet. Peace.

As Tom Wolfe described it in *The Right Stuff*:

> The X-1 had gone through "the sonic wall" without so much as a bump. As the speed topped out at Mach 1.05, Yeager had the sensation of shooting straight through the top of the sky. The sky turned a deep purple and all at once the stars and the moon came out—the sun shone at the same time. . . . He was simply looking out into space. . . . His was a king's solitude, unique and inviolate, above the dome of the world.[4]

Work with me here: I think we can experience something like this in our spiritual lives. Sometimes we'll be working, pushing, trying, all our bolts and screws rattling loose, shaking and heaving with the effort of trying so hard. Sometimes it just takes the courage of pushing our spiritual throttle higher than we think we can survive, *utterly trusting in Jesus*. And then, *boom!* Suddenly we're in that place of peace and stillness, no longer rattled and shaken.

"Therefore let us be grateful for receiving a kingdom that cannot be shaken, and thus let us offer to God acceptable worship, with reverence and awe, for our God is a consuming fire" (Hebrews 12:28–29 ESV).

28

{The Burden of Suffering and God's Radical Rest}

The will of God is never exactly what you expect it to be. It may seem to be much worse, but in the end it's going to be a lot better and a lot bigger.

ELISABETH ELLIOT, *Keep a Quiet Heart*

The sun is still there . . . even if clouds drift over it. Once you have experienced the reality of sunshine you may weep, but you will never feel ice about your heart again.

ELIZABETH GOUDGE, *The White Witch*

Earlier I said there are four burdens that human beings bear. As we've seen, the good news is that we don't have to carry three of them. Jesus can utterly deliver us from our sin and our shame, and He can also relieve us of the rules-mentality and performance treadmill of the shoulds.

But there's another load we carry, which I know you've been thinking about but you're too polite to say so. It's the burden of *suffering*.

There are so many types of affliction that we bear in this world, some for the short-term and some for the long run. If you have a child with disabilities or a debilitating disease, you probably haven't had a good night's rest since he or she was born. If you are a caregiver for an elderly parent, spouse, or friend with Alzheimer's or some other wasting disease, you are exhausted . . . and as you look ahead, the years to come will likely bring only increasing loss and toil. If you are dealing with unemployment, chronic pain, cancer, foreclosures, or the loss of a loved one or betrayal in a relationship you trusted, the ongoing pain is a weight that can barely be borne.

So many of us live with shattered expectations, knowing that we should trust God and fear not, yet still bearing the sad burden of lost dreams . . . single people hoping for a spouse . . . infertile women hoping for a baby . . . divorced people who never dreamed their hopes would be dashed . . . exhausted women who are trying to make sense of living with their husband's addictions . . . the list goes on and on.

If you think you are alone in your particular type of pain and burden, you are not.

One of the godliest women I know—a single mom with a grown son—has prayed in tears for years for her son who is far from the faith of his youth. She is a passionate student of the Bible, throws herself into all kinds of ministry for others, excels in her career, has a great big rollicking personality and just plain loves Jesus. But she carries the burden of her wandering son, and she does not know when that load will be relieved.

And the plain fact is that some burdens are *never* relieved in this life.

"Well, gee, thanks for sharing," you say.

But anyone who tells you that you just come to Jesus and He will deliver you from all your hardships is not speaking biblically. Those who preach a false gospel of *God-will-give-you-whatever-you-desire-if-your-faith-is-strong-enough* give followers of Jesus a bad reputation, like we are out of touch and outright annoying to the rest of the world. The picture that comes to mind is of believers floating, silly and gaseous, irrelevant, and somewhere up near the ceiling, like that famous tea-party scene in *Mary Poppins.*

Of course, God can do miracles of any kind. He can protect loved ones in war. He can give people great jobs in a horrible economy. He can bring wayward sons and daughters home, provide wonderful spouses for the single and sweet babies to the infertile.

I have seen Him heal Stage IV cancer so that a friend's dreaded scan was in fact clear and the doctor was speechless. I have seen Him draw ornery, unlikely family members to Himself. I've seen Him heal broken marriages and repair broken hearts.

God *can* do anything, and it is our job to pray earnestly, in faith, for Him to do mind-boggling miracles if it is His will.

But it is not always His will.

It seems that God deals with our suffering in three ways.

First, sometimes *He miraculously delivers us*. This is our favorite way. We'll call this Intervention.[1]

Second, and often, He doesn't change the situation, but *He changes us*. This is Inner Action.

And third, He acts in the *midst* of our pain and gives us rest and relief, usually through fellow believers. This is called Interaction.

Let's start with Intervention. Miraculous deliverance. This is what we all want. Think of the biblical account of the apostle Paul and his buddy Silas when they were thrown into jail in Philippi, a leading city in Macedonia, which was a Roman colony at that time.

It's a long story, but the summary is that Paul had healed a fortune-teller slave girl from the dark powers that made her able to see into the future. Her owners were furious because they could no longer use her for their financial gain.

So the slave owners started yelling, and then—just as if they'd been waiting offstage for their cue—an angry mob appeared. These angry mobs are all over the book of Acts, just waiting to get into the action. They started attacking Paul and Silas. The authorities arrived and appeased the crowd by tearing off Silas and Paul's clothes and beating them with big wooden rods, which were the sign of Roman authority and lethal indeed. Then our guys were thrown into the "inner prison" of the Philippi Incarceration Center—maximum security. They were bleeding, probably naked, and chained into stocks.

I love how the story unfolds. Around midnight, Paul and Silas are praying and singing hymns to God.

Can you imagine? They are half-dead, in terrible pain, but are warbling away, belting out the greatest hits from their Jewish hymnbook, connecting with the God who was so real to them that He was near even in really bad circumstances.

The Bible says, understatedly, "and the prisoners were listening to them." You bet they were. And on about the tenth verse of "Just as I Am," you can guess that most of them were ready to walk the aisle, if they could, and come forward in response.

Then, *boom!* There was a huge earthquake, the walls shifted, the doors flew open, and the chains unbolted. Everybody was set free.

Isn't it strange that all the other prisoners didn't just run away into the night? It seems they wanted to stick with Paul and Silas—maybe they wanted to hear more prison karaoke—and our brothers were staying right in that ruined jail. Then the jailer comes running in, calls for lights, hears the great story, and many come to faith in Jesus that night. (See Acts 16 for the whole wonderful tale.)

There are plenty of times in our lives when we are stuck in situations that imprison us one way or another. And yes, sometimes God intervenes with a miracle and sets us free.

Years ago I interviewed believers in a rural part of Cambodia who were surrounded one night by a crowd that wanted to kill them. They told me that suddenly a bright light shone all around them, and their attackers ran away into the night. Incredible.

But more often, God doesn't change our situation miraculously; *He changes us.* This is the second way He works in suffering. Inner Action.

I'm sure, after his jail earthquake scenario, the next time the apostle Paul was chained in prison, he was lustily crooning hymns at midnight, singing "Joshua Fit da Battle of Jericho" with all his might, just waiting for the walls to come a tumblin' down, down, down, down.

But it didn't happen.

Paul, who experienced all kinds of miracles, visions, and wild, supernatural assurances of the reality and power of God, also had to deal with problems that just would not go away. No amazing "health and wealth" deliverance for him. He dealt with relentless, chronic pain that God did not remove.

> In order to keep me from becoming conceited, I was given a thorn in my flesh, a messenger of Satan, to torment me. Three times I pleaded with the Lord to take it away from me. But he said to me, "My grace is sufficient for you, for my power is made perfect in weakness." Therefore I will boast all the more gladly about my weaknesses, so that Christ's power may rest on me. That is why, for Christ's sake, I delight in weaknesses, in insults, in hardships, in persecutions, in difficulties. For when I am weak, then I am strong. (2 Corinthians 12:7–10)

Interesting.

Paul was knocked off his horse, so to speak, and transformed on the day of his conversion on the Damascus road. But throughout the long years of his journey with Jesus, he was further changed—sanctified—bit by bit by bit. It's a long process, whether you're the apostle Paul or you and me. Pride and conceit had been a big problem for Paul before his conversion . . . and they were probably a constant temptation in his life that followed. Perhaps Paul's suffering was God's tempering mercy in his life, preventing him from pride that could have ruined his ministry.

We don't know. What we do know is that God uses suffering, even though we wish He wouldn't, to accomplish things in our lives that might not be achieved any other way.

Sometimes we may not see what He's doing at all. We may know in our heads that God works through suffering and that He prunes us through pain. Yet we may experience, like C. S. Lewis after the death of his wife, nothing but the deafening silence of God. Or sometimes, as Lewis also said, pain can be God's "megaphone," the means by which He shouts to us what we cannot hear when we're comfortable. And sometimes in suffering we may come to just a lifeless, dull ache—feeling nothing—and we therefore assume that God is doing nothing, that He's left the building, so to speak.

In that there is no easy answer, no cheerful platitude. There is just dogged belief in God and His promise that He will never leave or forsake us, even when all evidence to that fact feels contrary. There is just holding on. I love what Lewis said in *The Screwtape Letters*: that the devil's desire to lull and destroy us is never more in danger *"than when a human, no longer desiring, but intending, to do [God's] will, looks round upon a universe from which every trace of Him seems to have vanished, and asks why he has been forsaken, and still obeys."*[2]

I have a friend who is a missionary. Sarah married the love of her life, Hugo, had two small children, and was working with her husband in fruitful, wonderful ministry in the Dominican Republic.

One Christmas they were in the United States on furlough, and tall, athletic Hugo was getting ready to play basketball with a bunch of friends. Then, as he was sitting on a bench, changing his shoes and talking with his buddies, he slumped over. It was a brain aneurysm.

Sarah received a phone call. She raced to the hospital. Her twenty-eight-year-old husband was dead.

Some months after this tragedy, Sarah was back in the Dominican Republic with her children, back on the mission field. Even as she wept and told her whole story to a group of us, she was lit by a fire within. She talked about the suffering of shock, grief, loneliness, fear, confusion, horror. She had periods of questioning God's presence . . . and yet she said she had also never had a more intimate experience of the actual presence of Jesus.

Tears running down her face, she said to us, "Even though this suffering has been so hard, I feel like if you knew what this experience of knowing Jesus Christ and the fellowship of His sufferings has really been like, you would actually be *jealous* of me and my loss."

Humanly speaking, this kind of inner change in the midst of suffering is impossible. But this is what God can do when we come to rest in Him.

29

{Respite: The Rest We Give Each Other}

Some of us will not see pain as a gift; some will always accuse God of being unfair for allowing it. But, the fact is, pain and suffering are here among us, and we need to respond in some way. The response Jesus gave was to bear the burdens of those he touched. To live in the world as his body, his emotional incarnation, we must follow his example.

PHILIP YANCEY, *Where Is God When It Hurts?*

The third way that God bears the weight of our suffering is this: rather than miraculously intervening, He *provides relief in our sufferings through other people.*

This is called Interaction.

Usually the people who offer comfort when we are in pain are those who have been through suffering themselves. In 2 Corinthians 1, Paul wrote about this: "Praise . . . the Father of compassion and *the God of all comfort, who comforts us in all our troubles, so that we can comfort those in any trouble with the comfort we ourselves receive from God.* For just as we share abundantly in the sufferings of Christ, so also our comfort abounds through Christ" (verses 3–5).

The word used for "comfort" here has to do with the idea of resting in God's rule. It has to do with trusting in Him, even in pain and suffering. It has to do with a secure sense of God's presence and sovereign plan. Those who experience that degree of trust, belief, and comfort can then pass it on to others.

Like many other couples in recent years, we have come through employment challenges. Though job issues pale in comparison to what so many people endure, it was discouraging to have to carve into savings to deal with current expenses. For me, it was scary to think about the future, which would soon include three kids in college . . . how would we pay for it all?

I did not want this burden. I want us to never, ever have financial concerns. I want to win the lottery every day, except to win it I'd have to buy a ticket, and I can't do that because I don't think the lottery is a very healthy idea. You get the picture; not having our regular income was hitting me right in my vulnerable spot.

But as we slogged through the desert of that particular financial challenge, we experienced such comfort from friends in the body of Christ!

People who had gone through the same thing were the first to call. Things happened I couldn't have dreamed of, nor appreciated if I had not been in this slough. Friends actually paid for our son to go to a great Christian camp that we otherwise could not have afforded. Our dentist cut us a break on payments. Then a person I didn't even know at the time called and asked if she could take me on a missions trip to Africa with her.

I went.

And suffice it to say that in a needy country in Africa, I saw *true* poverty and need. I lived very briefly among people who had no access to clean water or sanitation, kids and families who were right on the brink of a cholera outbreak. Many had lost parents and other family members in tribal conflicts. Some young people, now with struggling families of their own, were actually the result of their moms being raped by murderous gangs. Some were refugees who did not have passports, papers, or identities. Their future looked bleak indeed.

All this and so much more put my own situation into perspective. I am embarrassed to say this, but I had fallen into the stupid trap of comparing my circumstances at home with other people around me in Washington, DC. Everyone around us seemed to have more than us. Yet in our little green suburb—perhaps like where you live—people are richer than the vast majority of the people in the rest of the world.

How are we rich?

We have food in the refrigerator. We have clothing. We have a safe, dry place to sleep, clean water to drink, and toilets. We take hot showers each day with scented soaps. We can worship at our church without fear of harassment, arrest, torture, or death. We have Bibles in every translation we could dream of, vitamins, and (hopefully) insurance in case something bad happens. We have medical facilities to treat our children if they get sick, schools so they can learn, and in our family, we all woke up this morning without a life-threatening disease.

My friend Burt was in a remote part of Ethiopia, visiting with believers there. He saw a little shed that was part of a church property.

"What's that?" asked Burt.

"That's the 'persecution house,'" he was told. "Whenever a family in our church comes under persecution, we bring them here to the shed so we can protect them and take care of them." Some members of the church, facing threats and opposition from local extremists, had lived in the shed for months at a time.

Burt just could not help but think of our comfortable lives as believers in America, where the need for a "persecution house" is an absolutely unknown concept.

But the point is that the believers rallied together. They supported each other and comforted others with the comfort they had been given in their own times of need and the vitality of a faith that says God is real and worthy to be praised and trusted, no matter what. The interaction of the body of Christ helped but did not remove the burden of suffering . . . but the support made the load more bearable.

We can do the same thing.

My wonderful friend Rosemary went through traumatic suffering when, as a young woman, she was brutally raped at gunpoint. She was a public figure—she had her own local daytime television talk show at the time, had been America's Junior Miss, and was married to a rising politician who went on to become a congressman and then a United States senator.

After the crime, Rosemary had to deal with intense feelings of fear, violation, and shame . . . usually with a smile on her face for the public. But over the years she experienced real healing and God's grace on her. She was able to move from an inner core of fear to a real sense of freedom.

Today Rosemary's husband is a university president, and Rosemary has a quiet, deep, ministry to many, many young college women who have been through sexual abuse, date rape, and all kinds of other ordeals.

Because of her own suffering, Rosemary has a "sixth sense" about the hidden traumas smiling young women conceal within. The brutal crime she endured so many years ago has become a touchstone for real healing for others. That doesn't lessen the ugliness of the crime itself. But because Rosemary has allowed her mind to be transformed by God's healing power, her experience of the crime today can be used for good. God wins.

When I introduced the topic of suffering, I mentioned the difficult burden of having a beloved child with disabilities. In my own family, I've seen and felt the ongoing weary load of care borne by my sister Gloria and my brother Walt, who both had children with disabilities. This burden is an ongoing weight with no light at the end of the tunnel.

Similarly, my dear friend Brenda Solomon's experience vividly shows such pain . . . and the hope only God and His people can bring to a lifelong challenge like this. Brenda's story demonstrates how we can give each other the gift of rest.

Brenda and her husband, Lon, had three great sons, and their lives were a flurry of baseball practices, soccer games, and youth group. As senior pastor of McLean Bible Church in the DC area, Lon was focused on preaching and serving the needs of a congregation that was growing to become a 15,000-person congregation.[1]

Life was busy, and it was good.

Then, at age forty, Brenda discovered she was pregnant. She and Lon were thrilled when the doctor told them they were expecting a daughter. Brenda dreamed of ballet class and shopping trips, slumber parties, and prom photos.

As Jill was born, the first words Brenda heard were Lon's: "Brenda, you got your little girl!"

Jill was a dream come true. Brenda brought her home to a pink room and little pink outfits. After three boys, Brenda was done with blue.

When Jill was three months old, Brenda was changing her diaper one day, and her arm started shaking. Jill's fist was clenched; her little arm trembled for about thirty seconds.

It happened again a few days later. A neurologist prescribed anti-seizure medication. But the seizures kept coming.

A few months later, when Jill was in her stroller, suddenly her head twisted to one side, her arms and legs started flailing violently, and her eyes rolled back in her skull.

It was her first grand mal seizure, and the beginning of the Solomons' nightmare.

The doctors could do nothing. Jill had more and more seizures. They were like brutal lightning storms in her brain, leaving her exhausted and afraid. Lon and Brenda desperately prayed for her healing. They felt like they were in a deep black maze with no way out.

On Jill's first Thanksgiving, she had nineteen grand mal seizures.

Incredibly, she was still hitting her milestones. She was learning to crawl, walk, and talk. She knew her colors. When she was in need, Brenda could hear her little voice calling.

But the seizures were burning out her brain. Helpless, Brenda and Lon watched Jill lose abilities she'd once had. Bit by bit, she lost her language. Then she only had two words left: *Mama! Dad-dee!*

"Oh God!" Brenda prayed. "Just let her keep those two words. Just those!"

But then Jill was fighting for her life. Brenda fought right along with her, pleading with God and the doctors for the life of her daughter. So it didn't matter so much when all of Jill's words finally slipped away.

Meanwhile the Solomons could no longer come to their three

boys' sports events or just take them out for pizza and a movie. Their lives revolved around Jill's fragile, declining health. They were physically, emotionally, and spiritually exhausted. Brenda cried all the time. The boys were hurting, but they didn't want to bother their mom and dad with their needs when Jill needed so much more.

One morning when Jill was two and a half, Brenda was sitting with her on the floor in her pink bedroom. She assumed she'd be having another seizure soon—she was always just about to have another seizure—and she knew she could help her better if Jill was on the ground.

Brenda played gently with her little girl, singing to her even as she wept.

"Oh Lord!" Brenda sobbed, "Will I *ever* stop crying?"

The pain of Jill's pain was overwhelming. There was no hope, no way out, just an endless, dark future of exhaustion and grief.

"God!" Brenda wept. "I am at the absolute end of myself! I don't know what to do. The only thing I ask is that You use Jill in a mighty way, because this hurts so much, and I don't want to waste this pain!"

Looking back, Brenda says it seems odd that she asked God to use Jill, not herself. After all, Jill was just a small, disabled girl; Brenda was the adult, the successful pastor's wife, the person whom God would logically use to do something.

But in Brenda's desperate prayer, she says she was finally giving up her own control of Jill's life to *God's* will for Jill. She was laying down her dreams. She somehow realized, in a fresh way, the biblical truth that God uses the weak things of this world to shame the wise. He uses small, broken things to accomplish His great and perfect purposes.

And that's what He was going to do through Jill.

A few hours after Brenda prayed in tears on the nursery floor, she received a phone call from Mary, a woman she'd never met. She told Brenda that God had told her to call. Through their conversation—which was mostly Brenda crying and Mary listening—Mary made a plan to organize some caregivers for Jill so Lon and Brenda could get some rest.

Brenda had never heard of respite, but that's what Mary gave her. When the caregivers started coming, Lon and Brenda finally got some sleep. With rest, they felt they were able to make better decisions. They felt they took better care of Jill. And they were able to spend time with their boys.

"Respite gave us hope," Brenda says today. "It changed our lives. I don't know where we'd be today if we hadn't gotten it. Lon says he doubts he'd still be in the ministry; perhaps our marriage wouldn't have survived. I doubt we could have weathered the storm of Jill's disabilities without the grace of God, *expressed through His people helping us.*"

What resulted from Brenda's prayer on the floor was not just respite, great as that was. Brenda and Lon realized that if they were experiencing such severe strains—even though they were plugged in to a community of caring believers—how much more so for families who didn't have a spiritual home or a network of friends who could help bear their burden?

They found out that the stresses on couples like themselves are huge. Eighty percent of couples who parent a child with special needs end up divorcing, and more than 60 percent of children with special needs stay with their families for the rest of their lives.

Brenda and Lon hoped that McLean Bible Church could spearhead something unique—a short-term, overnight respite center for children with disabilities. A beautiful place where kids could come, feel welcome, and have a great time . . . and their parents could feel at ease about their care and receive the gift of respite, whether they needed to spend time with their other kids, go on a date, or just take a nap.

So after much prayer over many years, and through the Spirit of God working in and through many wonderful people, Jill's House opened in the DC area in 2010. It serves families and their children with disabilities, regardless of their religious background. It does so in Jesus' name.

"I know the difference respite made in my life," Brenda says, "and I believe that through Jill's House, God is answering my desperate prayer on the nursery room floor, so many years ago. God can use the worst brokenness in our lives to accomplish His good purposes."

By citing the courage of Brenda and Rosemary, I don't mean to minimize the deep pain of their suffering. Sometimes well-meaning people can put a Christian happy-face sticker on brokenness or tragedy. In an effort to comfort people in loss, they'll formulize it, as if tragedy A happens so God can create outcomes B, C, D, and maybe even E if we're extra good . . . as in "maybe God allowed this to happen so people would come to know Christ through your witness."

When I was collaborating on *Choosing to SEE* with Mary Beth and Steven Curtis Chapman, they told me that so many people had done this in the aftermath of their five-year-old daughter's accidental death in their driveway. Maybe people didn't know what to say, so they said the wrong thing, like those who told the Chapmans that God had allowed their daughter's death so they could minister to other bereaved parents. To which Mary Beth would reply, with tears and the refreshing honesty of a broken heart: "Well, I don't want to minister to others; I want Maria back!"

Of course the Chapmans are the first to say that God can and does use even awful things for all kinds of good. They have opted to work hard to perceive His presence in all kinds of ways in the aftermath of Maria's death. But the point is that we need to move beyond the trite "Christianese" responses to the awful burdens that people bear. More often, people just need a hug and our presence, not our words. God can and does and will use all things for His good purposes, but what we can truly perceive here is so limited, veiled in mystery. We cannot perceive the spectrum of His will, for we see in too few dimensions and our perception is so limited to time, not the realm of eternity.

Yet this immense, incredible God most often provides comfort, not through miraculous feats, but through humble means. Like the friends who simply come alongside us to hang with us in our pain and give us a hug, the ones who show us that we are not alone. The beautiful thing about this is that in various seasons of our lives, sometimes we receive comfort . . . and sometimes we get to give comfort to others by helping to bear their burdens.

This is how the body of Christ—the community of believers—shows Christ's law of love in a broken, hurting world, and how we can give one another the sweet gift of rest.

30

{How to Get a Good Night's Sleep}

Unless the LORD builds the house,
those who build it labor in vain.
Unless the LORD watches over the city,
the watchman stays awake in vain.
It is in vain that you rise up early
and go late to rest,
eating the bread of anxious toil;
for he gives to his beloved sleep.

PSALM 127:1-3 ESV

There's so much to explore about the rich theological implications of this wondrous notion of rest. Spiritual rest, Sabbath rest, resting at the speed of sound, giving each other rest . . . ah, yes, you say, that sounds great . . . but as for me and my house, we also just want a good night's sleep. Could it be that God's cosmic rest also can calm our restless minds that spin like gerbils on a wheel, all night long? Can God soothe our sleep disorders and we'll all end up looking like those annoying happy people in Unisom commercials who leap out of bed in the mornings, full of joy and goodwill?

Charles Spurgeon, who knew a thing or two about clinical depression and long, hard nights, said this:

> I have lain awake at night, wondering whatever I should do in certain cases. And at last I have come to the conclusion that I could not do anything and that I must leave all with the Lord. . . . I have, sometimes, in the midst of great pain, sat up in the night and been afraid to go to sleep for fear I should lose the heavenly calm that I was enjoying.
>
> When I have left everything with Him and submitted myself absolutely to His sweet will, and had full fellowship with Christ, I have wondered what I could fret about if I tried. I have said to myself, "There is peace for me in Heaven. There is peace for me on earth. There is peace for me in the grave. There is peace for me everywhere."[1]

Then, says Spurgeon, in the night of restless sleeplessness, it's as if Jesus says, "Peace, be still!" as He did when He calmed violent storms. Peace comes, as well as the rest the world cannot begin to understand.

I know that in my own life, when I am lying awake, full of anxiety and envisioning doom—which I am really good at—if I *truly* practice what Spurgeon is talking about here, my anxieties will be eclipsed by a childlike sense of trust, and I sleep.

But not always. Yes, there are times when God wakes us up, we know not why, so that we might pray for others. We may not know the fruit of those prayers until we get to heaven, but sometimes He denies sleep to us for a while so that we might bear another's burden and lift up a dear loved one in need or pray for persecuted brothers and sisters on the other side of the planet.

I have a friend who pops awake every morning at 4 a.m. She believes the Holy Spirit wakes her up just then to pray, which she does for an hour, and then she slides back into sweet sleep. She is one of the most energized people I know.

A different friend, Sharon, told me she just could not sleep one night. Frustrated, she got up and resolutely picked up a book to read. Sharon turned to the page where her bookmark was, and there was a reference to an overseas ministry that cares for orphans. Her daughter, a Spanish major planning to take a semester off to do missions work, had been looking for just such a thing.

Sharon felt strangely warmed. She got online at 3 a.m. to research the ministry, felt like it was a perfect match for her daughter, forwarded the info, and went back to sleep. And as I write, her daughter is in Costa Rica, serving with great joy and blessing in that very ministry.

I *know* that God can give supernatural sleep to His beloved. He doesn't always, for reasons only He knows. But He can. The most dramatic example of this that I've ever seen was in Rwanda, when I went there a few years ago and interviewed Christine, a new friend who had survived that country's horrific genocide.

You recall that back in 1994, the world stood by in shock and appalling inaction when conflict erupted in Rwanda. Like many African nations, it had its history of upheaval, civil war, and tribal or clan conflict between the majority Hutus and the minority Tutsis.

As anyone who has traveled to Rwanda knows, it's very difficult for Westerners to analyze its politics and history in a way that rings true across the board with Rwandans. There's no generalization that does justice to the horrors of the genocide and its aftermath. I spoke with Hutus whose loved ones were killed as well as Tutsis whose loved ones were killed. Since 1994, there have been incredible stories of healing, growth, and reconciliation in Rwanda . . . as well as stories of ongoing anger and pain.

The genocide itself began in April 1994. Dark forces took over the country after the assassination of its president, and over the course of three months, nearly one million Rwandans were killed by other Rwandans. In the beginning, most of the attacks were carried about by clan militias that had been organized for months. These were made up of extremists of the Hutu tribe; their goal was to eradicate the Tutsi tribe—they called them "cockroaches"—whose members had held a more privileged role in Rwandan society.

The marauders also killed Hutus who wanted peace and tolerance, UN peacekeeping troops from Belgium, minority clans in the country, and anyone who stood in their way. Most of these victims were slaughtered by murderous groups of young men wielding machetes; they hacked their victims to death and mutilated men, women, and children alike.

On the night of April 6, madness descended on Rwanda, starting in the capital city of Kigali. Radio broadcasts fanned the flames of violence and hatred: ordinary citizens were advised to stay in their homes . . . where they would be easier to isolate and kill. Moderate government officials were assassinated. Civilians who sought sanctuary in churches were massacred.

Militia members set up roadblocks, demanding identity cards. If your tribal designation—or the way you looked—did not please them, you would be dragged out of your car and murdered right on the roadway. Students at suspect schools were killed. Babies and toddlers were cut into pieces. Neighbors rapped on the doors of neighbors and killed whole families. Women were raped and men were dismembered.

This went on for 100 days of horror, until Tutsi forces eventually took control of the country. At that point two million Hutus—some guilty, many innocent—fled the country in fear of Tutsi retaliation. Many, many died of cholera and dysentery, as well as random revenge killings.

That is the backdrop of Christine's story.

Christine's husband was a church leader, well known in the country. Christine was a spiritual leader as well. She and her husband had planted churches, worked with Compassion International, started Bible studies, and enjoyed the great fruit of growing groups of believers all over Rwanda. They had a big home church in Kigali and eleven other daughter churches.

In April 1994, Christine's husband happened to be out of the country, along with their two children. Christine had been unable to join them because of her job at the US Embassy.

When the horror began, Christine was trapped in her home. She could not believe what was happening. Armed militias of young men wearing fatigues and red, black, green, and yellow scarves roamed the streets. She could hear gunfire, thuds, shouts, and screaming.

As the days went by, occasionally she'd hear scraps of information whispered through a window. In one of their daughter churches that had seventy members, only the pastor's wife had survived. The rest were dead.

One night she could hear a boy in the street crying, "I'm dying. Please, come pray for me. I don't want to go to hell!"

The killers were still out there.

Better to die a physical death than a spiritual death, Christine thought.

She ran out to the street. The boy was lying on the pavement. Blood everywhere. She knelt and prayed with him, holding his hand, and stayed with him until he died.

A militia gang crowded around. She was caught. This was the end.

"Ha," one of the gunmen said. "Let her go. Wait until tomorrow. We've already shed so much blood today."

Incredibly, they let her go.

Days and weeks went by. Christine had no way of knowing then, that hundreds of thousands of people had already died. There was no way to escape. The roadblocks were everywhere.

"Oh God!" Christine prayed. "You made a way for Moses through the Red Sea! You can blind the eyes of enemies!"

Up until this point, she had somehow been able to catch an hour of sleep here and there, patching together catnaps that, mixed with terror and adrenaline, had kept her going. But now, though she was restless and exhausted, she could not sleep.

She prayed. She was terrified of being hacked to death, as so many of her friends had been. She could not stem the fear of bleeding to death, slowly pouring out her life on the street.

But then she had a vision, a sense of Christ's death on the cross. She knew that the forces that were operating in Rwanda weren't just political but far deeper: they were spiritual. *For politics you cannot slaughter a baby*, she thought. *That is of Satan.*

She saw in a new way the spirit of ethnicity and prejudice that was fueling the hatred of the murderers. She saw how the enemy—Satan—had come to Rwanda to steal and destroy. But God's Son could give life. "Oh Lord, have mercy on Rwanda!" she cried.

She saw before her Jesus on the cross, pleading for mercy for His killers. She sensed the weight of her own sins, the power of His forgiveness. She prayed for a "holy revenge" to come to Rwanda . . . that God's Spirit would *triumph* over the prevailing spirit of evil. Then, Christine told me, "I felt innocent, like a baby." She lay down and slept a deep sleep of peace.

Christine later escaped through the help of a Hutu friend. She went out to the street. She went through roadblock after roadblock; all had been abandoned by the machete-wielding troops that had slaughtered hundreds of escaping people.

"God made a way," she told me, "a resting place" in the midst of chaos.

She slowly made her way to freedom. And she and her husband and family press on in great ministry in Rwanda today.

Of their home church in Kigali, left in rubble, it turned out that three-quarters of the people were slaughtered during the early days of the genocide.

"Why them and not me?" Christine says today. "They were better people than me."

Can God cause a woman like you or me to get a good night's sleep while bloodthirsty killers roam the streets, butchering innocent people?

Yes. Yes, He can. It is all about seeing Him, lifted up on the cross, more powerful than the dark forces Satan may let loose around us. It's also about understanding that this life is not all there is.

Christine's story is a beautiful story of survival in the midst of obscene horror.

But what about the people from her church who were not miraculously rescued? What about all those other believers, all across Rwanda, who were killed during the genocide and after? What about *them?*

Ah. They went Home.

31

{Ultimate Rest: Coming Home}

We bring our years to an end like a sigh.
The years of our life are seventy,
or even by reason of strength eighty;
yet their span is but toil and trouble;
they are soon gone, and we fly away.

PSALM 90:9–10 ESV

Better is the end of a thing than its beginning . . .

ECCLESIASTES 7:8 ESV

In death, a follower of Jesus experiences the ongoing climax of Jesus' invitation in Matthew 11.

Come to Me, and I will give you rest!

However we experience that last moment of life on this earth, the next breath is with Him.

Tragically for some, like those brothers and sisters in Rwanda, the last seconds are full of pain and chaos. For others, there's not even the knowledge that the moment has arrived, as in the case of a brother in Christ who was a victim of the DC sniper some years ago. One moment he was pumping gas, the next second his body was on the pavement, a bullet in the brain—but he was catapulted right into the presence of Christ.

For many, the decline toward death is slow, uncertain, yet inexorable, and then there you are in hospice . . . perhaps alert, perhaps in a coma, perhaps in a narcotic state due to pain-relieving drugs.

All of us have loved ones who've made this journey. Whether their departure from this realm was sudden or slow, accidental or because of some horrific crime, pain-filled or pain-free, it is a mystery to those of us who are left behind.

My mother was a lovely, pink-cheeked, silver-haired, slightly eccentric believer in Jesus. My friends often say that her eccentricities came to me in spades. I say to them, "Hey, what about the loveliness?" They usually remain silent.

But anyway, as my mom got older, she would often say to me, "I think death must be the most *exquisite* experience."

I didn't know what she meant when I was younger, but now it's beginning to make sense.

When I walked with my mother down the path toward her final journey, and even as I watched her die, I couldn't imagine what it was like for her. I didn't see anything exquisite. But I believe that she did.

Maybe it's like a new birth . . . you're stressed, pressed, in a dark place, and then all of a sudden you pop out of the birth canal into a place of light and wild, fun activity.

Or maybe it's like that scene in C. S. Lewis' *The Last Battle*, when the last Narnians are in the final conflict with the forces of evil. Narnia's young King Tirian is fighting, focusing on the battle around him. He loves his friends deeply and is dimly aware that in the course of the battle, they are going down all around him, one by one by one.

But in the darkness and the fray he is distracted, fighting for his life. All is sweat and confusion and tears and blood. He is fighting, fighting, and then, "For a moment or two Tirian did not know where he was or even who he was. Then he steadied himself, blinked, and looked around. He was in strong light."[1]

Tirian finds himself in a place where his friends are all around. But they're not weeping, dirty, and bloodied as they were in the course of the battle. They are fresh and clean, laughing, welcoming. They take him to meet others who have come ahead of them. They must go farther in, and higher up . . . and the Adventure begins.

Hospice nurses tell us that it is common for people who are near death to speak in metaphors. A dad who loved sailing all his life might well talk about "setting sail" or heading out with the next tide. An old soldier might issue orders that it's time to stand down. A mom might be concerned that her suitcase is packed and by the front door.

Though the apostle Paul wasn't yet dying when he wrote these words, I like his imagery. A longtime tentmaker, he described the human body's death like this: "For we know that if the earthly tent which is our house is torn down, we have a building from God, a house not made with hands, eternal in the heavens" (2 Corinthians 5:1 NASB).

As Erwin Lutzer says in his book *One Minute after You Die,* "Our present body is like a tent where our spirit dwells; it is a temporary structure. Tents deteriorate in the face of changing weather and storms. If used regularly, they often need repairs. A tattered tent is a sign that we will soon have to move. Death takes us from the tent to the palace; it is changing our address from earth to heaven."[2]

If our journey as believers is from the tattered tent to the palace, death is simply the taxi that takes us straight to Him. Believe me, I'm not making light of death or minimizing its pain, suffering, and obscene evil. Death is not noble or good; it is a result of the Fall, and will be banished forever, right along with sin and Satan, at the end of all things.

But I am saying, yes, for the follower of Jesus, death is a taxi, the means by which we get to our destination.

I thought of this recently as I stood by the deathbed of a loved one and watched his taxi come to take him away to that place of rest.

My ebullient sister Gloria is twenty-five years older than me. Our mother was married at seventeen and had Gloria at age eighteen. Twenty-five years later, at age forty-three, she gave birth to me, clearly the pinnacle of her childbearing efforts. (Just kidding, Glo!) We have a brother and a sister between us, age-wise.

Gloria was married by the time I was born, and when I was five she moved to Southern California. She raised her family and has lived there ever since, while I've remained on the East Coast. Though we are separated by many years and many miles, we've become deep, true soul-sisters who have supported one another through all kinds of things. We have similar loves and passions and deeply held opinions. We laugh at the same twisted things.

For example, I received this email from her not long ago.

Ellen:

BE AWARE! Gold is at an all-time HIGH! $1500 per ounce!

Please know that I have EIGHT (8) gold molars! When I die, have them removed before consigning me to the crematorium!

As I do not feel so well, you must be ALERT!

Don next door says for a tiny token of the take, he will use his pliers for the above-mentioned items, before the ambulance arrives.

Love & Kisses,
Gloria

Gloria's husband of more than fifty years, Chan, was a loving, steadying influence throughout her life. He loved Jesus, but because his life and testimony were less dramatic than Gloria's, we didn't tend to focus on Chan as much. I think he liked it that way.

A year ago Chan's health declined. It gradually became clear that he was on his way to glory. I traveled to California and got to spend two weeks with my sister . . . an unprecedented time of prayer, praise, tears, and bonding.

On a sunny Saturday, Chan was lying in his hospital bed in their bedroom. His breaths were shallow. He hadn't eaten or drunk anything for days. The hospice nurses felt his time was soon.

At about noon Gloria and Chan's pastor arrived. A few other friends were there as well. We gathered around Chan's narrow bed, holding his hands, stroking his shoulders. Gloria was on one side of the bed; I was on the other. We kept looking at each other, and at Chan. Was it now?

Pastor Ray began reading from the end of the book of Revelation: *"Then I saw a 'new heaven and a new earth' . . . And I heard a loud voice from the throne saying, 'Look! God's dwelling place is now among the people, and he will dwell with them. . . . He will wipe every tear from their eyes. There will be no more death or mourning or crying or pain, for the old order of things has passed away.'"*[3]

Tears rolled down our faces and dripped on the sheets. Chan's skin was tight across his bones, his closed eyes sunken, his handsome face so thin and old.

"*He who was seated on the throne said, 'I am making everything new!'*" Ray continued.

Another labored breath. "It's okay, darling," Gloria whispered. "Your work here is done. You can go! The kids and I will see you there later! You can go!"

"*Then the angel showed me the river of the water of life, as clear as crystal, flowing from the throne of God and of the Lamb down the middle of the great street of the city.*"

Chan's mouth was open, and parched. He was so dry. Another hard breath. Was it the last?

Ray read on.

"*The Spirit and the bride say, 'Come!' And let the one who hears say, 'Come' Let the one who is thirsty Come; and let the one who wishes take the free gift of the water of life.*"

We looked. We waited. No more breaths. Silence.

Chan was gone; only his shell was left behind. We couldn't see it, but he had somehow flown away from us . . . to *come* right into the actual presence of Jesus—sitting with Him, staying with Him, reveling in the ultimate rest . . . the joy and glory of coming Home.

Of course, even as Chan slipped away from this shadow-land to the concrete reality of heaven, we could not see what he was seeing. We couldn't taste the fresh water of life or dance on the golden streets or laugh in the land without tears. We were jealous, in a way. Same old, same old for us, while Chan was flying farther in and higher up, loving the new Adventure with Jesus.

So the challenge for those of us left behind, until our own taxi comes, is to truly *see* with the eyes of faith, and to anticipate what we don't yet know.

Earlier generations did this better than we do. Early martyrs of the church mystified—and converted—onlookers by their bravery in the arenas of Rome. They knew, even as they were torn apart by wild animals, that heaven was just a breath away.

Pilgrims and saints with hard lives talked a lot about entering into their "final rest." In this I can't help but think of the journal of David Brainerd, missionary to native Americans in the Delaware Valley in the 1730s and '40s. He was a vibrant personality full of love and life, yet also weary of this world, sometimes depressed. He worked hard in difficult, dangerous circumstances, and he often longed for heaven.

One fine April day, he wrote in his journal:

Oh! there is a sweet day coming, wherein "the weary will be at rest!" My soul has enjoyed much sweetness this day, in the hope of its speedy arrival.

He mourned over the shoulds:

Appeared to myself exceedingly ignorant, weak, helpless, unworthy, and altogether unequal to my work. It seemed to me that I should never do any service, or have any success among the Indians. My soul was weary of my life; I longed for death, beyond measure. When in thought of any godly soul departed, my soul was ready to envy him his privilege, thinking, "O, when will my turn come! Must it be years first?"

About six months later he wrote:

Oct. 31. Oh! I thought, if I could but be spiritual, warm, heavenly minded, and affectionately breathing after God, this would be better than life to me! My soul longed exceedingly for death, to be loosed from this dullness and barrenness, and made forever active in the service of God. I seemed to live for nothing, and to do no good: and Oh! the burden of such a life! Oh! death, death, my kind friend, hasten and deliver me from dull mortality, and make me spiritual and vigorous to eternity![4]

In spite of his melancholy—or perhaps because of it—David Brainerd labored faithfully among the Indians until he died of tuberculosis at age twenty-nine. Given the passionate nature of his writings, it's not surprising that his journals spurred on a young man two centuries later who longed to bring the gospel to Indians on a different continent.

In October 1949, a vigorous young Brainerd fan named Jim Elliot wrote in his journal, "He is no fool who gives what he cannot keep to gain that which he cannot lose."[5]

Jim Elliot went on to determine that a violent, unreached tribe in Ecuador needed to hear the gospel. After much prayer and preparation, he and four friends flew into the dense jungle, bearing gifts. They came in peace. They did their best. And because of tensions and conflict within the tribe, the missionaries were speared, cut, and killed. Though Jim Elliot wore a gun, he did not use it to defend himself. He and his colleagues had determined that it was better for them to die than to send those who did not yet know Jesus into a Christless eternity.

Interestingly, the very men who speared the missionaries ended up coming to faith in Christ. They are old men now. And they look forward to worshiping God in heaven with those who died to bring them the gospel.[6]

At any rate, great saints, old and new, saw heaven rather differently than many of us today. Perhaps we're too comfortable or distracted; heaven just doesn't have the cachet it did for earlier generations. In fact, if we're honest, heaven sounds like a real snoozer.

As the wonderful and witty Randy Alcorn says in his great book *Heaven*, many of us think of eternity like one of Gary Larson's *Far Side* cartoons. A man with angel wings and a halo sits on a cloud, alone, with nothing to do. The caption shows his inner thoughts: "Wish I'd brought a magazine."

Well, *Far Side* aside, heaven is actually a place of glorious fun. Not to get too dramatic about this, but I think the common cultural images—benign and boring mental pictures of flaccid cherubs, harps, and plump clouds—are used by Satan to lull us to sleep. If we had the actual astounding reality of heaven in our hearts and minds, we'd be wild, radical believers the world could not stop . . . kind of like the early martyrs. We would live with abandon and die with smiles on our faces. We'd know the reality of Hebrews 2:14–15, which says that since human beings share in flesh and blood, Jesus Himself took on flesh and blood, that through death He might destroy the one who has the power of death—the devil—and "deliver all those who through fear of death were subject to lifelong slavery" (ESV).

We'd automatically be better stewards of our time here on earth. We'd have more peace in the midst of suffering and tears. We'd grow less weary in well-doing, knowing the ultimate rest lies just beyond the finish line.

Ah, and what *is* that ultimate rest?

The former English slave trader who was saved and transformed by Jesus, John Newton, talked a lot about heaven's rest. I think he was tired.

Ah, sighed Newton, *rest!* Absolute rest from worry and guilt and the yapping tiresomeness of our own works. Rest from the gross effects of sin all around us. Rest from pain, tears, sorrow. Rest from unsatisfied desires. Rest from Satan's temptations. And, of course, rest from all sin.

"We shall be free from sin in ourselves," said Newton in an eighteenth-century sermon on Matthew 11:28. "This alone would be worth dying for!"

We can define the great rest, like Newton, by what is not in heaven. No frustrations, addictions, anxiety, or gut-churning fear. No confusion, no bitterness or rage. No boredom. No tears. No inadequacy, jealousy, or comparisons with others. No sin, no shame, no shoulds, no suffering.

Even more powerfully, we can focus on what heaven is.

Can you imagine?

Well, no, we can't, because we just see dimly at this point what will later be absolutely clear: the laughter of the heavens, the magnificent dance of the Father, Son, and Spirit—the dance in which we too will spin and step in glorious grace.

One of the key distinctives of this rest will be our altered experience of time. Theologians and philosophers argue about whether God exists in a land beyond time, in "divine timeless eternity," or "timelessness and omnitemporality." Or is it "unqualified divine temporality"? Or "relative timelessness"?[7] We don't know. But for those of us who aren't philosophers, it's helpful to think of the pleasure and freedom of dwelling in God's *present.*

In heaven we will not regret the past nor fear the future. We will not look ahead, anxiously wishing for things that are not yet, nor look back in sadness to things that have passed us by. We will have come to rest, stopped, simply being in the moment, in the wonderful "today" of Jesus' presence.

I've always been struck by the account of Jesus' words to the repentant thief who died right next to Him. The guy was a bandit, a bad dude, but hanging there on his cross, he realized that he was guilty and deserved punishment. He also recognized that Jesus was innocent and righteous.

"Jesus, remember me," he rasped, "when You come into Your kingdom."

"Truly I tell you," said Jesus, when every breath was torture, "*today* you will be with me in paradise" (Luke 23:43).

Men who were hung on crosses typically took several days to die, which is one reason it was such a feared form of execution. But Jesus knew that the bandit—and He Himself—would both be dead before the end of that day. But they'd be together in a place He called Paradise.

The word appears several times in the New Testament. The apostle Paul used it when he spoke of his glorious visions of heaven . . . revelations that gave him freedom to hold on to this life loosely. The word comes from the old Persian term *pairi-daeza*. This means a walled garden, a place of beauty, blossoms, fragrance, and exquisite pleasure and delight. It takes us back to the original Garden of Eden, located in the ancient Persian fertile crescent between the Tigris and Euphrates Rivers.

The Bible story, and our story, is framed by two perfect gardens. It began with Eden: Paradise lost. It culminates in a never-ending ending—in Paradise regained—because of Jesus: Revelation's glorious garden of rest.

Obviously, I'm not trying to lay out a thorough theology of heaven in these pages. But I believe that the Bible is clear about two things: first, when believers die, we are immediately in the presence of Jesus. And second, the new heaven and the new earth to come will be glorious, physical places that we will enjoy in really cool resurrected bodies. Maybe we'll revel in the best surfing, hiking, climbing, walking, picnicking, skiing, swimming, and tubing. Perhaps we'll play tag on Mars, or gallop on glorious white horses on the beaches of a renewed Hawaii. We'll float on our backs in the River of Life. We'll jam with jeweled hummingbirds and feast with the apostle Paul, all those multiple Marys of the Bible, and Abraham, Martin, and John. We'll rap with the more rhythmic angels and sing in glorious harmonies with the heavenly host and people from every tribe and nation . . . all to the glory of God, and utterly free of the tawdry junk of competition, jealousy, and measuring ourselves against others.

We'll have full, perfect freedom in which you and I thrill with the inexpressible pleasures of magnificent delights, belly-laugh on the golden shores, and bow with perfect praise and absolute thanks to the One who made us, saved us, bought us, and brought us back to His garden of abundant rest.

This is where we're headed.

> Then the angel showed me the river of the water of life, bright as crystal, flowing from the throne of God and of the Lamb through the middle of the street of the city; also, on either side of the river, the tree of life with its twelve kinds of fruit, yielding its fruit each month. The leaves of the tree were for the healing of the nations. (Revelation 22:1–2 ESV)

The One who sits on the throne calls to us, *Come!* He sits enthroned in heaven because His work is done, done on our behalf so we can *sit* with Him, *stay* forever . . . and *rest* with Him the way He planned from the very beginning.

Ahhh. *Come to Me, all you who are weary and burdened, and I will give you rest!*

{Notes}

CHAPTER 2: ROYAL INVITATION, LEGAL SUMMONS, RADICAL RESCUE

1. C. S. Lewis, *The Great Divorce* (New York: Macmillan, 1946), 72–73.

CHAPTER 3: WHO IS THE MASTER?

1. John MacArthur, *Slave* (Nashville: Thomas Nelson, 2010), 14–15. As MacArthur puts it: "We don't hear about that concept [of being Christ's slaves] much in churches today. In contemporary Christianity the language is anything but slave terminology. It is about success, health, wealth, prosperity, and the pursuit of happiness. . . . [God] wants to fulfill every desire, hope, and dream. *Personal* ambition, personal fulfillment, personal gratification—these have all become part of the language of evangelical Christianity—and part of what it means to have a 'personal relationship with Jesus Christ.' Instead of teaching the New Testament gospel—where sinners are called to submit to Christ—the contemporary message is exactly the opposite: Jesus is here to fulfill all *your* wishes. Likening Him to a personal assistant or a personal trainer, many churchgoers speak of a *personal* Savior who is eager to do their bidding and help them in their quest for self-satisfaction or individual accomplishment. The New Testament understanding of the believer's relationship to Christ could not be more opposite. He is the Master and Owner. We are His possession. He is the King, the Lord, and the Son of God. We are His subjects and His subordinates. In a word, we are His *slaves*."

2. William Ernest Henley, poem originally untitled in *A Book of Verses* (London: David Nutt, 1888) but later titled "Invictus."

3. http://blogs.telegraph.co.uk/news/danielhannan/100021943/invictus-the-inspiration-for-nelson-mandela-timothy-mcveigh-and-now-gordon-brown/

4. http://abcnews.go.com/Entertainment/charlie-sheens-craziest
-quotes/story?id=13028952

5. Charles H. Spurgeon, sermon delivered June 7, 1891; *Spurgeon's Sermons* (Grand Rapids, MI: Baker Publishing Group, 1996).

CHAPTER 4: JESUS CALLING

1. Mark Dever illustration, cited by John Piper in "Jesus, Islam, Pharisees, and the New Perspective on Paul," December 6, 2006; http://www.desiringgod.org/resource-library/taste-see-articles/ jesus-islam-pharisees-and-the-new-perspective-on-paul

CHAPTER 7: COME OUT OF YOUR BUSH!

1. Joseph Hart, "Come, Ye Sinners, Poor and Needy," 1759.

CHAPTER 8: THE BURDEN OF SHAME

1. Rape, Incest, and Abuse National Network; http://www.rainn.org/ statistics

2. W. D. Rogers, "Shame-full vs. Grace-full Relationships"; http:// ccame.org/shame_grace.html

CHAPTER 9: THE BURDEN OF THE SHOULDS

1. Vickie Abeles, *Race to Nowhere: The Dark Side of America's Achievement Culture* (Lafayette, CA: Reel Link Films, 2010); http://www .racetonowhere.com/

2. This helpful material is from Jeff VanVonderen's books, *Families Where Grace Is in Place* and *Tired of Trying to Measure Up*, as cited by W. D. Rogers in his online article "Shame-full vs. Grace-full Relationships"; http://ccame.org/shame_grace.html

CHAPTER 11: THE SHAME BREAKER

1. The Old Kingdom Pyramid Texts of Dynasties 5 and 6 (Pharaohs Unas, Teti, Pepy I, Merenre Antyemsaf, and Pepy II, ca. 2375–2184 BCE) mention the deceased Pharaoh as a Golden Calf born of the heavens (in Egyptian myth, recalling that the heavens were seen as a cow goddess—either Hathor or Nut—giving birth to the sun at dawn); http://www.bibleorigins.net/EgyptianOriginsGoldenCalf .html

CHAPTER 12: THE BURDEN BREAKER

1. Charles H. Spurgeon, sermon delivered January 30, 1859; Emmett O'Donnell, "Spurgeon Gems & Other Treasures of God's Truth," http://www.spurgeongems.org

2. See "Bono: In Conversation with Michka Assayas"; http://www.thepoachedegg.net/the-poached-egg/2010/09/bono-interview-grace-over-karma.html

CHAPTER 13: HOW YOUR SQUISHY LITTLE BRAIN CAN HELP YOU

1. Curt Thompson, *Anatomy of the Soul: Surprising Connections between Neuroscience and Spiritual Practices That Can Transform Your Life and Relationships* (Salt River, 2010.) Curt's website is http://www.beingknown.com/

2. http://en.wikipedia.org/wiki/Neuron

3. Thompson, 64.

4. Ibid., 74.

5. Ibid., 72.

6. Ibid., 77.

7. C. S. Lewis, *The Complete Chronicles of Narnia* (New York: Harper-Collins, 1998), 118.

CHAPTER 14: IT'S EPIDEMIC

1. Thanks to George Guthrie's thoughtful blog of January 13, 2011, "Spiritual ADD & the Skill of Focus"; blog.georgeguthrie.com/?p=291

2. Quoted in "Pay Attention Please," by Christine Rosen, *Wall Street Journal* online, January 7, 2011: http://online.wsj.com/article/SB10001424052748704440570457606490027907050.html. "Neuroscientist Brian Knutson imagines a near future in which 'the Internet may impose a "survival of the focused," in which individuals gifted with some natural ability to stay on target, or who are hopped up on enough stimulants, forge ahead while the rest of us flail helpless in a Web-based attentional vortex.'"

3. Guthrie, "Spiritual ADD."

CHAPTER 15: BE STILL

1. John Piper, "God Works for Those Who Wait for Him," sermon delivered September 5, 1982; © Desiring God. Website: desiring God.org
2. Ibid.
3. Ibid.
4. For more about the idea of "I can't, but He can," see Dick Woodward and Ellen Vaughn, *The Four Spiritual Secrets* (International Cooperating Ministries, 2009), http://www.icm.org/online_store/

CHAPTER 17: "LEARN FROM ME"

1. C. S. Lewis, *Mere Christianity* (New York: Macmillan, 1943), 56.

CHAPTER 18: SIT DOWN AND COUNT THE COST

1. Aron Ralston quotes are from Aron Ralston, *127 Hours: Between a Rock and a Hard Place* (New York: Simon and Schuster, 2004).
2. Timothy J. Keller, "Greed: The Case for the Rich Young Ruler," sermon delivered on March 19, 1995; http://sermons2.redeemer .com/sermons/greed-case-rich-young-ruler
3. Michael Warner, "Why Gay Men are Having Risky Sex," *Village Voice,* January 31, 1995.
4. Charles H. Spurgeon, sermon delivered February 22, 1874; *Spurgeon's Sermons* (Grand Rapids, MI: Baker Publishing Group, 1996).
5. John Piper, *Desiring God: Meditations of a Christian Hedonist* (Portland: Multnomah Press, 1986), 194-95.

CHAPTER 19: SIT DOWN AND GAIN YOUR RIGHT MIND

1. Shana Schutte, "Conquering Cutting and Other Forms of Self-Injury"; focusonthefamily.com/lifechallenges/abuse_and_addition/ conquering_cutting

CHAPTER 20: SIT WITH FRIENDS

1. C. S. Lewis, *The Four Loves* (New York: Harcourt Brace Jovanovich, Inc., 1960), 126.

CHAPTER 21: KEEPING PACE

1. Francis Schaeffer, *The Finished Work of Christ: The Truth of Romans 1–8* (Wheaton, IL: Crossway Books, 1998).

CHAPTER 23: UNLEASHED!
1. Dwight Pentecost, *Design for Discipleship* (Grand Rapids, MI: Zondervan, 1971), 27-28.

CHAPTER 24: JESUS, STAY WITH US!
1. G. K. Chesterton, *Orthodoxy* (Rockville, MD: Serenity Publishers, 2009), 138.

CHAPTER 25: THE REST OF THE STORY
1. Ray C. Stedman, "Jesus Is Our Sabbath Rest"; http://www.ldolphin.org/sabbathrest.htmlRay
2. Ibid.
3. Timothy J. Keller, *King's Cross: The Story of the World in the Life of Jesus* (New York: Dutton, 2011), 43.
4. Stedman, "Jesus Is Our Sabbath Rest."
5. Timothy J. Keller, "The Rest-Giver," sermon delivered February 20, 2005.

CHAPTER 26: FREE AT LAST
1. C. S. Lewis, *Mere Christianity* (New York: Macmillan, 1943), 190.
2. Charles H. Spurgeon, sermon delivered November 2, 1856; found on Emmett O'Donnell, "Spurgeon Gems & Other Treasures of God's Truth," http://www.spurgeongems.org

CHAPTER 27: FUN REST
1. Oswald Chambers, "The Graciousness of Uncertainty," see http://www.sermonindex.net/modules/newbb/viewtopic.php?topic_id=28565&forum=45&2
2. Ibid.
3. Charles H. Spurgeon, sermon delivered March 5, 1893; *Spurgeon's Sermons* (Grand Rapids, MI: Baker Publishing Group, 1996).
4. Tom Wolfe, *The Right Stuff* (New York: Farrar, Straus, Giroux, 1979), 58–59.

CHAPTER 28: THE BURDEN OF SUFFERING AND GOD'S RADICAL REST

1. I am indebted to Pastor Todd Phillips for these three points, which I scribbled on a napkin in my Bible during a sermon at McLean Bible Church during the summer of 2009 or 2010.

2. C. S. Lewis, *The Screwtape Letters,* rev. ed. (New York: Macmillan, 1982), 39.

CHAPTER 29: RESPITE

1. This particular account of Brenda's journey is based on our conversations in the fall of 2009. Parts of this account appeared in a letter I assisted Brenda with; it went to Jill's House supporters at the end of that year. To find out more about Jill's House, visit their website at www.jillshouse.com.

CHAPTER 30: HOW TO GET A GOOD NIGHT'S SLEEP

1. Charles H. Spurgeon, sermon delivered March 5, 1893; *Spurgeon's Sermons* (Grand Rapids, MI: Baker Publishing Group, 1996).

CHAPTER 31: ULTIMATE REST

1. C. S. Lewis, *The Complete Chronicles of Narnia* (New York: Harper-Collins, 1988), 505.

2. Erwin W. Lutzer, *One Minute after You Die* (Chicago: Moody, 1997), 53.

3. See Revelation chapters 21 and 22.

4. *The Diary of David Brainerd* is available through a variety of sites online. I used http://www.eternallifeministries.org/brainerd.htm

5. For the Billy Graham Center archives selection from Jim Elliot's journal in his own handwriting, see http://www2.wheaton.edu/bgc/archives/faq/20.htm

6. See Steve Saint's compelling book *The End of the Spear* (Carol Stream, IL: Tyndale, 2005), in which he chronicles his return to the Ecuadorian jungle and his friendship with the tribe members who took his dad's life when he was a small boy, before they came to faith in Christ.

7. For a provocative discussion of these topics, see *God & Time: Four Views,* ed. Gregory E. Ganssle (Downers Grove, IL: InterVarsity Press, 2001).

{Acknowledgments}

With Gratitude

I am most deeply grateful to God for the gift of breath in my lungs, grace in my life, and a computer that works. I am also so thankful to Him for the many wonderful human beings that He's given me to live life with, and for their patience and support in my writing endeavors!

THANK YOU:

Lifelong BFF Patti Bryce, as well as Sharon Hubbard, Carey Keefe, Laura Warren, Bobbie Wolgemuth, and Joy Zorn, who read the initial chapters of this book and let me know if I was halfway coherent or not.

Mary Ann Bell, the Reverend Carleton Bakkum, Ed Bethune, and Gloria Hawley, who read parts of the manuscript and offered insights as I wrote. Dr. Curt Thompson, for sharing his insights from *Anatomy of the Soul.*

Paul and Rosemary Trible, for hosting me in your beautiful home for a very productive writing retreat. Thank you for so lavishly welcoming the "crazy aunt in the attic."

Friends and sisters who let me share their stories: Gloria Hawley, Brenda Solomon, Rosemary Trible, Christine Gatabazi, and so many others.

For miscellaneous encouragement and prayer support along the way: Norma Vaughn; Holly Leachman; Jerry Leachman; Janice Allen; supper club (Jim and Laura Warren, Scott and Sharon Hubbard, John and Susan Dawson, Tom and Tracey Pilsch, Rich and Lisa Hannibal, Jeff and Nancy LeSourd); the Heart, Soul, and Mind group at McLean Bible Church; Joanne Kemp and the "Friday Class"; Andi Brindley—early mentor and friend for decades . . . soon I will be older than you!; Greg and Cathe Laurie, who rooted for *Come, Sit, Stay* as the title; Randy Alcorn, for his contest of wittiness with Greg and his insights on heaven; Carl and Mildred Santilli, who now live in heaven but blessed me immeasurably during their time down here; Jamie Longo, for sharing your rich faith and love for Rwanda with me; SCORE retreat women, who let me try out early ideas on them as guinea pigs; and everyone involved in Christ's work in the Dominican Republic.

Gus Vaughn, who lay on my office floor as I wrote and loved it all, even though his furry brain is the size of a peanut.

Steven Curtis Chapman, for your creative camaraderie and your very gracious foreword!

Michelle Rapkin, for your editing skills and thoughtful solidarity.

Byron Williamson, Rob Birkhead, Jeana Ledbetter, Kris Bearss, Sherrie Slopianka, Morgan Canclini, and the rest of the fun, talented Worthy team, as well as Kelly Hughes, for your public relations help!

My dear friend and literary agent, Robert Wolgemuth, wonderful Bobbie Wolgemuth, and the handsome colleagues at Wolgemuth and Associates: Andrew Wolgemuth, Erik Wolgemuth, Austin Wilson, as well as Susan Kreider.

Emily, Haley, and Walker Vaughn, who heard me talking to myself at the computer, did not question my mental health, and encouraged me enormously and hilariously along the way.

Lee Vaughn, who gives me the gift of rest and the secure joy of partnering together for a lifetime!

I dedicated this book, in part, to Chuck Colson when I finished the manuscript several months ago. I looked forward to sharing my dedication, and the final printed book, with him after its release.

Sadly, Chuck died this afternoon. I miss this man: boss, father, mentor, colleague, brother with a warped sense of humor . . . an influence on my life for whom I will be eternally grateful. But of course, as Chuck was fond of quoting, C. S. Lewis said that Christians never have to say "Good-bye." So I will see you later, old friend, and thank you!

Lastly, thank you, reader, for reading! Anyone who peruses a "with gratitude" section has got to be a dedicated Book Person. May the Lord bless you and keep you and make His face to shine upon you, and give you peace . . . and rest for your soul!

Amen.

ELLEN VAUGHN
April 21, 2012
Reston, Virginia

Ellen Vaughn collaborated with Mary Beth Chapman, wife of Steven Curtis Chapman, on her *New York Times* bestseller *Choosing to SEE,* and coauthored various award-winning books with Chuck Colson. She also collaborated on the *New York Times* bestseller *It's All about Him*, the story of Denise Jackson, wife of country music superstar Alan Jackson. Vaughn's solo books include *Time Peace, Radical Gratitude,* and *The Strand.* She lives in a Washington, DC, suburb with her husband, Lee, their three teenagers, and two dogs.

WORTHY
P U B L I S H I N G

IF YOU LIKED THIS BOOK . . .

- Tell your friends by going to: http://www.comesitstaybook.com and clicking "LIKE"

  - Share the video book trailer by posting it on your Facebook page

  - Head over to our Facebook page at facebook.com/worthypublishing, click "LIKE" and post a comment regarding what you enjoyed about the book

  - Tweet "I recommend reading #Come, Sit, Stay Book by @EllenSVaughn @Worthypub"

- Hashtag: #ComeSitStayBook

- Subscribe to our newsletter by going to http://worthy publishing.com

WORTHY PUBLISHING
FACEBOOK PAGE

WORTHY PUBLISHING
WEBSITE